Other Li… es

BOOKS

by Rev. Thomas A. Hensel & Rev. Kevin Ross Emery

Experiment: Earth

The Lost Steps of Reiki: The Channeled Teachings of Wei Chi

TAPE SERIES

by Rev. Kevin Ross Emery & Rev. Thomas A. Hensel

The Channeled Messages of Simon Peter

The Lost Steps of Reiki: Transforming An Ancient Healing Art

Prosperity & Manifestation

TAPED LECTURES

by Rev. Kevin Ross Emery & Rev. Thomas A. Hensel

Bridging The Gap: Christianity In The New Age

Combing The Mirror

Empowerment: Taking Back Your Life

Invisible Armor: Protecting Your Personal Energy

What Is Wei Chi Reiki?

COMBING

THE

MIRROR

(and other steps in your spiritual path)

Rev. Kevin Ross Emery

Forward by
Rev. Thomas A. Hensel

First edition, 1998

Published by:

LightLines Publishing
1 Middle Street
Portsmouth, NH 03801

E-mail: LightLines@weboflight.com

Manufactured in Canada

ISBN 1-890405-20-5

Illustrations

Screen Beans™ from http://www.bitbetter.com

Screen Beans is a registered trademark of *A Bit Better Corporation.*

ACKNOWLEDGMENTS

It is so difficult to figure out how to thank all the people you want to thank and somehow saying "Thanks, everyone" just does not quite do it. So here are a few people that I would like to acknowledge:

Papa: There is so much of you in me that it is hard to know when I am giving one of your answers or one of mine when people ask me questions.

Fran Bolduc: To my first mentor, my deepest sympathies. I still have not had a student that put me through the paces that I put you through.

Erma Mae Ross Emery: My grandmother, who gave me so much by saying so little. And who introduced me to a loving God who gives gifts, not grief.

Hazel Stevens: My other grandmother, who taught me to have an open mind and to keep living and growing to at least one day after you are dead.

Thank you also, to all of my students who had the wonderful talent of bringing issues to me that I most needed to work on myself. The teacher learns from the students as much as the student learns from the teacher.

Contents

This book is lovingly dedicated to:

Rev. Thomas A. Hensel,
life partner, business partner and the person who was exactly what I asked Spirit to send me.
You help me apply my wisdom to myself and keep me honest, adding new levels of happiness every day of my life since you entered it.

Foreword

by Rev. Thomas A. Hensel

As we move forward, exploring our own lives and opening up our expansion as spiritual beings, we all look back and take stock of our lives. We remember those moments and instances that were pivotal, life-affirming, sometimes life-shaking. Many were obviously transformational while others were subtler. It is to one of the subtle ones that I personally trace my most powerful life transformation.

One evening, late in July 1995, I was sitting at my computer exploring what was, to me, the new world of the Internet. In a chat room, I was discussing some minor aspect of astrological chart interpretation, when a quiet beep caught my attention, followed by the appearance of an instant message window.

The message was simple. It read, "Hi! My name is Kevin." From that unobtrusive beep has come the most powerful transformations in my life. In that moment, I first made contact with Rev. Kevin Ross Emery. Shortly thereafter, we became business and life partners, forging a union that has been life changing for both of us.

We all draw teachers into our lives, both obvious and subtle. Kevin has played both of those roles, and many in between for me. In return, I have served in that capacity for him. Undoubtedly, we have both learned and taught much to each other. One of the most powerful lessons I have learned from Kevin, however, is the primary lesson embodied in this book. It is the message of SIMPLICITY.

We laughingly refer to our philosophy as K.I.S.S. The acronym stands for KEEP IT SPIRITUALLY SIMPLE. Frankly, if you cannot take information and apply it to your life today in order to move forward more joyfully, then what is the point? As a species, we humans have a fundamental tendency to complicate our lives. We clutter up our minds and our physical spaces with unwieldy amounts of information. As a result, our emotional lives become complicated and, ultimately, our spiritual lives transform into a mirror image of the mess we have created in all other aspects of our being.

Kevin, in his work as a counselor and in this book, has developed techniques and perspectives which seek to dig beneath the surface of the complications to uncover the simple truths which govern our lives on all four levels: physical, emotional, intellectual and spiritual. In reality, the creation of complication is a smoke screen, an attempt to cover what we do not wish to see. We are a society of escapists, and our greatest place of denial is in our spiritual lives.

No doubt, there are truths in every system, no matter how complex or convoluted it may seem. The point to realize, however, is that no other person or system has your personal truth. Each person has a truth ... their truth. Your personal truth is constructed from bits and pieces of everything you have experienced in your life. In essence, your path is constructed from pieces of every other path you cross. Each person has some part of your path for you. The trick is to recognize and embody those pieces in your own life.

This book, simply and profoundly, offers tools to teach you how to recognize and utilize those pieces of your path. Kevin has created a system, which can help to transform your life by teaching you how to reconnect with those simple truths which have been covered up by years of conditioning.

Kevin and I jokingly refer to this process as “learning to body surf on the flow of life.” May this book help to make your body surfing effortless and a constant source of joy as you learn to live, rather that simply surviving. My life has been transformed by the simplicity and power of Kevin’s approach. It is my fondest desire that you, too, allow these truths to become the bits and pieces of a new path for you. A path towards joy and empowerment.

Live life .... don't let life live you! Namasté!

Rev. Tommy Hensel
November 24, 1997

I have known since I was four that I have certain "gifts," what my paternal grandmother called my "gifts from God." But it took me close to thirty years of exploration, discovery and denial to come to terms with those gifts, as well as their purpose in my life. Sooner or later I was bound to stumble onto the facts that through these "gifts" a great deal of healing could be facilitated, and that the sharing of these gifts through teaching and individual work could bring me great joy. As soon as I "gave up" all the "suppose to's" and owned my own power, amazingly enough, I stopped being the master of the merry-go-round and the king of justification. I finally stopped fighting and started accepting. Now, every day I get up knowing in some way I will make the world a better place than I found it, if I just allow myself to be me. Some days allowing is easier than others; however, on those days I interfere and stop just 'being," I eventually get around to reminding myself that when all else fails, just keep breathing.

Even though my grandmother told me that I had the gift, I waited until I was fifteen to start actively working with my first mentor, Fran Bolduc. By the time I was twenty, I had done everything from past life regressions, hands-on healing, and working as a psychic, to clearing haunted houses. I had some knowledge of everything from Astrology to Zen.

Amazingly enough, it was during this period that I came to

realize I would know whatever I needed to know whenever I needed to know it. How did I come to that understanding? Fran would give me books and would send me home to read them, and then would speak with me on a number of related topics, all of which I could comment on, sometimes from several different perspectives, even though I had read none of the books! Poor Fran. It used to really rile her, being the avid reader she was. At this time she quite often referred to me, not as “Kevin,” but as “You little shit,” one of my fonder nicknames. Like a sponge, I absorbed much from the people that came in and out of my life through Fran. I did not work to expand my gifts or even strengthen them. Actually, I ran as fast as I could from them so I could be “normal”.

In my late twenties I took independent study courses at the Association of Research and Enlightenment (ARE), Edgar Cayce’s legacy. There I found what I needed to start full-time work with my gifts with a realization of the larger soul of which I am a part.

In my early thirties, after twelve years in the corporate world, I began working with Dara Jane Brennan and we created our own business, New Moon Visionaries, later renamed Spiritual Concepts. It was during my association with Dara that all the information I have channeled and my natural inclination toward healing and teaching merged. This resulted in my ordination as a minister in the Universal Brotherhood Movement and my full-time dedication to helping other people find and walk their own spiritual paths. In my mid-thirties, I received very strong messages to go on the road, where I spent three years of my life. During this time, I expanded a great deal as a trance channel, published two books, (*The Lost Steps of Reiki* and *Experiment: Earth*), produced three audiotapes (*The Lost Steps of Reiki*, *Prosperity & Manifestation* and *The Channeled Messages of Simon Peter*), created a new business and picked up a new business/life partner. Not bad for living on the road full time.

The purpose of this book is to share the one-on-one teaching and counseling that my partner Rev. Thomas A. Hensel and I do with our students to assist them in reaching enlightenment, recognizing and following their own spiritual paths and learning how, through this process, they can become more empowered. I have yet to find power <u>without</u> enlightenment that has not been power based on fear or scarcity. No matter how much of that kind of power you have, it leaves you hungry and always wanting more. Never satisfied. That is not empowerment.

There are exercises throughout this book which contain many of the homework assignments that I give my students. Doing the exercises and assignments will assist you in your search for empowerment and enlightenment by helping you grasp and integrate the information in this book.

To paraphrase Plato, "there are no new ideas, only new ways of expressing them." So there is nothing new in this book. But it might be new to you, or put in a new way, making it more usable to you. My greatest hope for this book is not that it becomes a best seller, but that it becomes a book people read, understand, and use to create a better life for themselves. The success of this book will not be measured by how many copies it sells, but by how many people it helps to empower. Namasté.

Rev. Kevin Ross Emery
July 1997

COMBING THE MIRROR

(and other steps in your spiritual path)

Welcome to student work. Through this process you will discover how to look at your past, your present, and your future in such a way as to see your soul's purpose and feel empowered to, without apology, be the best that you can be and take full accountability and responsibility for your life. Remember, the only thing you are responsible for is to be the best you that you came here to be. This book can only give you the tools for this transformation. You must use them. Unlike one-on-one teaching, this book is unable to "call you" on any inconsistencies between your stated goals and your actions. Therefore, if you have someone in your life who is willing to work with you, to be honest and to accept honesty, I suggest you work with them in pairs or even groups. I also offer personal assistance to those who desire it. Either in person or via phone, I (or one of the coaches trained personally by me) will help guide you through the homework, adding additional work and altering the existing exercises to fit your individual needs. Please see the note on page 136 for more information.

A willingness to want to do things differently is paramount. One definition of insanity is "to do as you have always done and to expect a different result." If you and your friend(s) have read every new "spiritual" book out there, praised, talked about, recommended and shelved them, and you do the same with this book without doing the work, then thank you for your money . . . even if you have just wasted it!

The first thing I express to students is my purpose for doing this kind of work and my expectations of those students. I am a healer, and only a healing energy will come to me and through me. I pursue student work with the intent of awakening the healer that lies within each student and to help them discover their own spiritual path. I do this in the hope that by each student becoming a teacher and passing on the healing, they will spread the light in an ever-growing ripple effect and cover the world.

Part of my drive to do this has been the disturbing channeled messages I have received concerning our choices here at this time on this planet. The earth changes are coming, but are not written in granite. We can change the amount and severity of those earth changes, but the only way we can do so is through the increase of positive spiritual energy on the planet. This is not simply a stated awareness, but an awareness that is reflected by action. It has also been made quite clear to me that there was no way I can do this work alone. Mine is to teach and heal, allowing my students to bring forth the teacher and healer which lies within each of them.

In private sessions, at this point, I ask my student to agree to the following two criteria, and I ask the same from you. I ask you to actualize your own healing energies and to be willing to share those energies with the world. If you can make these commitments please stop at this point, take a moment, close your eyes and offer this up to Creator. I may not know if you have done this but you, the Creator and Mother Earth will, and that is all that is important.

Now that you have made a commitment, a commitment to yourself, we can continue. The first things you need to understand about discovering your spiritual path are these: it is yours and you need to take ownership of it. That is a double-edged sword. Each person's spiritual path is as individual as each person is. We will go over how you came to choose that path later, but understand that no other person's way is yours. There is no universal right way. There is no universal only way. Visualize your path like a twisting, turning cobblestone path. As you go through life, you pick up stones of different shapes and sizes, which fit your personal path. One of your stones may be Judeo-Christian, another might be Buddhist. One might be formed by being a parent, another by being a child.

As you accept your path as your own, you must also accept the fact that you have brought into this path everything you need to follow it to where you want it to go. And the traveling is the process of how you choose to grow through the experiences you have manifested. As you accept full accountability and responsibility for the things you have brought into your life, you must do it for ALL things you have brought into your life.. You cannot do this student work and be a victim. You cannot blame your parents, your spouse, your children, or anyone else for your unwillingness to grow. You can only blame your own fears: fear of the unknown, fear of claiming your power, fear of being more than you've ever been or even dreamed you can be. You can examine your fear of failure, your fear of success or even your fear of leaving other people behind, but you cannot blame those people or anyone else.

You also cannot hold onto those old patterns: not being good enough, bright enough, or beautiful enough. If you do, then you will not succeed at utilizing the tools in this book. You will yet again live through the self-fulfilling prophecy, and you will not be good enough, only because you told yourself so and chose to believe it. And believing it was just that - a choice.

If you can accept the responsibility for all you have brought into your life and you can leave behind your victim status, we are ready to begin. We will also include work on negative self-patterning and victim issues. They're hard habits to break and may need to be done in steps.

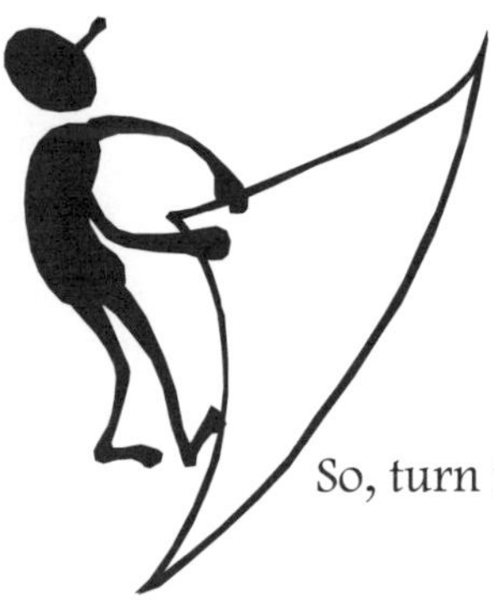

So, turn the page and let's go!

The secret of applying all this wisdom to your life will be through what my students have come to truly hate: HOMEWORK. Homework refers to those assignments that I give to you which require you not only to think, but to do some work. Now I know that <u>work</u> is a four letter word, but if you thought for the price of this book I was going to do all your work for you, then you're crazy! So as you go through the book, you will find the heading HOMEWORK at the end of certain chapters. All I would like to do at this point is give you a few insights about how to be most prepared.

1) Get a large loose-leaf notebook and a couple of packs of 500 sheets of filler paper. (Yes, you can get less but if you don't use it all you will find other things to do with it. And if you run out in the middle of a real flow of self-discovery you will kick yourself!)
2) Get a package of ten dividers
3) Buy three or four writing instruments that you really enjoy using and set them aside for use with this notebook. For you computer addicts, you can do all this on your handy dandy computer but be prepared and knowledgeable about how to use split screens.
4) Get a set of color-coded index cards.

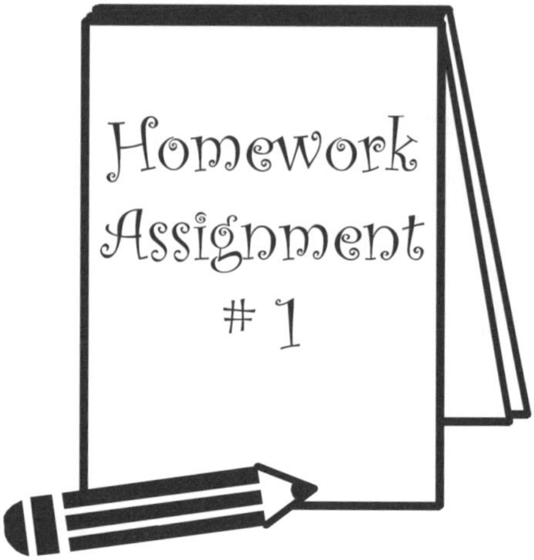

CREATING YOUR PERSONAL WORKBOOK

With the dividers and paper, create these sections to begin with:

A: OUTFLOW WRITING
B: DREAM JOURNAL
C: DREAM INTERPRETATION
D: MESSAGE LOG
E: HOMEWORK-CURRENT
F: JOURNAL
G: PERSONAL SYMBOLOGY
H: LETTERS
I: HOMEWORK- COMPLETED
J: MISCELLANEOUS
K: BLANK PAPER

Now that you have done your first homework assignment, we can start putting it to use. First I recommend that you commit at least five minutes every day to outflow writing. By outflow writing, I mean allowing yourself to get in a relaxed state of mind with no expectations as to what you are going to write. You just put pen to paper and let it flow. Now the first several times you do this you may be resistant and feel unprepared or even stupid trying to write from a blank mind. That's okay. What I suggest is that you begin by writing your concerns, whatever crosses your mind. You can start any writing- "I feel foolish I have no idea what I am going to say I hate doing things like this" but just keep writing. The more you practice, the more likely you are to have things just suddenly "appear" in your writing. These may be messages from God, your higher Self, a spirit guide, or Uncle Marty, who died last year and wants to give you a good horse to bet on in the fifth (never knock where Spirit may gift you with abundance). Before you do this, however, I do recommend an intention and protection statement. If you do not have one, use this one: "I am only open to messages and energies that are for my highest and best good." Just so you don't get some joker saying he is Uncle Marty and you end up losing your shirt at the track!

Also, begin keeping track of your dreams. Later in the book we will spend some time on basic dream interpretation but it is a good habit to get into now. That way you will have some material to use when you get to that chapter.

When I refer in future homework to the idea of journaling- that differs from outflow writing because then you are engaging your intellect and emotions to help accomplish some breakthrough on a particular issue. Some people journal on a daily basis as a way to keep their emotions and thought from getting too built up. It also gives them clarity. If this idea appeals to you, then by all means do it. I make this more optional because of the great many HOMEWORK ASSIGNMENTS that you will be getting in addition to the daily dream log and outflow writing assignment.

Part of searching for those stones that fit your path is to be discriminating about which stones to use. Remember, you may only choose part of someone's philosophy, whether that someone is a person, a church, or an author. So let's start right here. As my student you need to understand first of all, you cannot have my path, because it's mine. But while you walk alongside me on my path you are welcome to take what you want and leave the rest. I do not believe I have THE way nor do I look to have incense burned at my altar. Take from our time together what resonates to you. Perhaps what does not resonate now, will later. Maybe it never will, and that's okay too. Now, if I say something that you've heard before, maybe, just maybe you need to look at it again. You might have just a wee bit of resistance to something you know you need to do but do not want to do. That is yours. Just remember, that which we resist, persists.

Next, it is time to get that word out and discuss it. I call it Spirit. I do not care if you refer to It as God, Goddess, the Universe, the Creator, the Collective Unconscious, Jesus, Buddha, Allah, Spirit, the White Light, or the Great Pumpkin. It is the intent with which you say it, not what you say. Each and every one of those words has been used with purity and with perversity. Personally, I think God sits up there elbowing the closest angel saying, "See what they are calling me today, how cute." If the spirituality you are exploring to incorporate in your life uses any of those words as justification for hate or judgment, you may want to walk (run) the other way. Be assured, it is not from Spirit.

As we begin our adventure, think of it like a great detective game. You have been getting clues from your moment of conception and will get clues until the moment of transition (death). Please realize you do not need all the clues to figure it out. So we divide life into three parts.

Past: Including past lives, the transition into this life, and your past in this life
Present: How to start doing the things you need to do today and every day to get a firm hold on your path.
Future: How to stay centered, on your path, and consciously create a harmonious future.

It is very frustrating to work hard to get to your path, to understand and integrate your past, only to find out a couple of years later that you did not stay on it, but just intersected it and now have to start the process all over again. You usually start again from your point of intersection, not from birth, but it is still backtracking and a pain, so why do it? Besides, there is a reward, but to hear about the reward you'll have to keep reading. Before you can go any further, you need to understand a couple of terms and ideas that can work for you or against you, depending on how well you learn to work with them. So, let's move on to something new, or at least previously uncovered: ELF, Ego and Belief Systems (BS).

To explain how to work with your ELF and your EGO to maximize your life, we need to begin with a working definition of what we mean. EGO is your unique expression of Spirit. Belief systems (BS) are those ideas which you were trained to believe from earliest childhood. Many times we were indoctrinated with these to the point, where not to follow them would effect everything from finding true love and being accepted by everyone, to our immortal soul. We were conditioned and forced into becoming pasteurized and homogenized versions of whatever belief systems our environment dictated. Our individual uniqueness was only promoted as long as it was within the comfort zones of our caretakers. We many times have redefined what we refer to as ego by what I refer to as Belief Systems, which is not our unique expression of spirit, but our reactions to the world through the eyes of conditioning, which is often either fear-based or comes from ignorance. This is why people will often refer to the ego as that which is meant to protect us from extinction, and is tied to our animal-based instincts. We do have animal-based instincts and they are part of our individual expression of Spirit. As I explained in my earlier book Experiment: Earth, that is from the animal connection we, as souls, created prior to our having bodies at all.

We are taught the most desirable condition is one where we are in control, of situations, emotions, desires, etc. The reason our BS needs to "control" so much is because control is an illusion, as is the majority of what our belief systems were constructed from originally. Also remember the EGO is the way we apply the messages from Spirit, which has very little to do with control. But as we have been further and further separated from the God within ourselves, we have trained the BS to take on a bigger and bigger role in our life. We have been trained to listen less to our *gut* instincts and more to what our logical mind is conditioned to believe. The rate of suicide may be so high today because of an EGO/BS which has become short-circuited with the overload of responsibilities that it was never meant to have.

Then we have ELF. First, let's clear up the image of a little person who lives in the woods. In this book, ELF is an acronym for *Essential Life Force*, and that is simply your inner connection to the Universe. This direct line is supposed to give you the guidance you need to live your daily life, follow your life's path and fulfill your soul's purpose. Ideally, by the time you reach adulthood, you should function with greater than 90% ELF. So, how did we get so far off track? As the spirituality we received from established religions fell ever more victim to a need for control, we began to believe less and less in the church and became more and more afraid of both the questions and the answers. As doctrine became more important than the spirituality itself, we moved into the age of reason with "logical" and fear-based doctrine becoming our God. The important thing at this point, however, is how this process happens in our lives today and how we can reverse it.

When we are first born, we may still be sorting out things from our last incarnation. As babies, we dream and have nightmares, and as the memories fade back into the subconscious, we move into the business of survival all over again. As we learn basic survival skills (what's hot, how to walk, how to fall down, etc.), we have little fear. The EGO is being trained and developed, as it should be. Around four to five years old children have very thin veils and are very in touch with their ELF-self. The highest number of recorded spontaneous past-life recalls is with this group. They are also sensitive to ghosts, auras and other psychic abilities. At this point, most parents respond to these abilities with comments like, "You have such a vivid imagination." "Didn't I tell you not to lie?" "What do you mean you see colors around me? There must be something wrong with your eyes." "No, there are no such things as ghosts, only Santa Claus and the Easter Bunny."

Or even worse: "If you see or know those things, then you are evil and the devil is working through you." This sets up the first stages of not believing in yourself, not trusting your instincts and the beginning of a lifetime full of mixed messages. Or of being scared to death of some eternal damnation. This is how we slowly started hammering down the ELF and replacing it with the fear-based EGO, which is becoming more and more BS.

As we subject our children to BS concepts such as win/ lose, prejudice and scarcity, we keep building the BS and beating down the ELF. Most of the institutions to which we subject our children speak in black and white. They use dog collar terms to interfere with the children's ability to trust themselves and to be themselves. Dog collar terms are those terms which indicate judgment. They are spoken in absolutes and are used to keep people in line or on a leash. These terms are very prevalent in our culture when we say something is black or white, good or evil. These and many more are used to make us fall into obedience with the thoughts and beliefs of the institution (church, school, society, family) that wants to be in control. Our children grow up either not believing in or trusting anyone else, or trusting someone else too much. Our children are stripped of the ability to love, trust and believe in themselves and then we wonder why they feel and act in a self-abusive or unempowered way. In fact, we have participated in stripping from them the ability to love, trust, and believe in themselves.

It's time to examine some of the basic differences between ELF and the Belief Systems with which we have been indoctrinated. Part of our work is to learn how to determine when EGO is giving us information and when we are getting it from ELF. Remember, EGO in its purest form is an expression of your uniqueness. It is not a doctrine, dogma or set moral code; often, however, what is reacting to any given situation is from the BS we were taught.

IDENTIFYING WHERE YOU ARE PASSING ON THE JUDGEMENT

Make a list of "dog collar" terms that you grew up with, terms or ideas that were used to "keep you in line" or on the "straight and narrow". Examine each one that comes to your mind and journal about what each of them meant to you then. What were your feelings and thoughts about them? Are they still valid for you? Do you still react to them when you hear them? Do you use them on yourself, other people or even on your own children or spouse? What would life be like without them? Is it time to release them? If so, then create a word or phrase that has positive energy and every time you start to use the old ones, replace it with your new one.

Now, let's take a look at some Belief Systems and expand on them with insights offered by ELF!

ELF & Belief System CHART

BELIEF SYSTEM	ELF
You have winners and losers. Choose which you want to be.	Every situation has a win/win solution.
There is a limited supply. You have to get yours before the other person gets theirs.	There is more than enough of everything to go around. There is no need for scarcity.
It is a love/hate world. I will only love you if you love me the way I want.	All souls are loveable. It is the actions which you dislike. Love without expectations.
Everything is good luck or back luck. It is because of an angry or vengeful God. When things go wrong, it is always someone else's fault. If it goes right, it is because you are good.	Everything happens for a reason. Understand that the messages involved can allow your life to run more peacefully. You have control.
Judement	Discernment
Choose sides, either you are with me or against me.	We are all on the same side.
It's best to always maintain a rational, analytic mind.	Intuitive inner voice.
Fear everything you don't understand.	There is no fear.
You need to control everything in your life.	You have no control over anything but your free will.
Hate change and feel threatened by it.	Accept change as an opportunity.
Impatient, always feeling hungry, but often not knowing for what.	Satisfied with the pace with which things unfold, feeling full.

Let's expand on the chart in more detail, exploring what fears might dwell within the Belief Systems.

BELIEF SYSTEM

You have winners and losers. Choose which you want to be.

FEAR

In order for you to be a "winner," someone else must be a loser. Fear also comes from the idea that the purpose of life is "get to Heaven," giving no credit to the process of the journey.

BELIEF SYSTEM

There is a limited supply. You have to get yours before the other person gets theirs.

FEAR

This often times comes from a fear of scarcity, the idea that there is not enough to go around, also the fear of coming up short when being compared. In the western world it is often not as much a case of "getting enough to survive" as much as "getting as much as" everyone else is getting.

BELIEF SYSTEM

It is a love/hate world.
I will only love you if you love me the way I want.

FEAR

That you are unlovable and anyone who says that they love you must prove it, and because you are inherently unlovable, or not good enough, or bad, the only way to feel at all lovable is to find and point out people who are more unlovable than you.

BELIEF SYSTEM

Everything is good luck or bad luck. It is because of an angry or vengeful God. When things go wrong, it is always someone else's fault. If it goes right, it is because you are good.

FEAR

This can be either fear of an angry God or the need to be a victim, then it's always somebody else fault.
This also stems from a fear of responsibility.

BELIEF SYSTEM

Judgment.

FEAR

Of being judged, and found lacking.

BELIEF SYSTEM

Choose sides, either you are with me or against me.

FEAR

That you do not deserve loyalty, or a lack of belief in what you are doing and saying, or even a need for external validation.

BELIEF SYSTEM

It's best to always maintain a rational, analytic mind.

FEAR

Being rational and analytic is often seen as being logical, therefore right. For men, there can be a fear of it being "unmanly" to be emotional. Also, that being emotional is a weak, inappropriate or unstable way to make decisions. It also keeps you blocked from your intuitive.

BELIEF SYSTEM

Fear everything you don't understand; control everything in your life, or hate change and feel threatened by it.

FEAR

These three constructs are very closely related and usually come from thc following fears:

* A fear of the unknown, and what you don't know can hurt you.

* A resistance to look at new things because it may lead you to questioning your belief system and the security on which you have based your life.

* Fear of being unable to handle change or unpredictable events; coming up against a challenge and failing.

BELIEF SYSTEM

Impatient, always feeling hungry, but often not knowing for what. Either a need to 'rock the boat' or living out a belief that you must be a 'bad' person to have an exciting life.

FEAR

This comes from knowing there is more than that which you have been allowed to experience, combined with a fear of eternal punishment for "breaking the rules" or questioning the belief system.

This is by no means a complete list of possibilities but these will be somewhere in the thought process, conscious or unconscious, more often then not.

FINDING YOUR BELIEF SYSTEMS & FEARS

Examine the list of Belief Systems and see which ones into which you most often fall. Keep track for one week of all the different times you fall into one of those and react to a situation based on them. Then journal about each incident and see if you can see the connection between the disempowering belief system and the fear which was connected to the reaction.

NOTE:

Just a quick note on Belief Systems and ELF. When we go over the things you need to work on today, in the "Present" section of the text, we will again spend time on ELF and EGO, learning how to develop the proper balance of each in your life. Before we leave this section, however, I do want to distinguish between the ELF's gut feelings and true emotional feelings.

Listening to your heart often is listening to your emotions, not your ELF The majority of emotions are fear based: fear of harm, fear of abandonment, fear of looking foolish, etc. We get emotional because of our fears. ELF has no fears. What is not from fear is from love and even that is tricky because only if it is from unconditional love is it from ELF. A good way to judge if a message or feeling is from ELF is this: if it will intentionally hurt anyone else or yourself then it is not from ELF, it is also not from Spirit.

From this point on, stop as you receive feelings and messages. Also, stop when you try to make decisions, and see if you can identify if the information you are getting is from ELF or BS. At this point, just try to make yourself more aware of your own inner thought processes. The first real step after making the decision that you want to change is to get in touch with the why and how of what you are doing now.

One last thing before we start the hard core work. Consider this chapter the warning label on the side of the package. By doing this work, you will open Pandora's box. The following items will probably fly out at you as you open this lid. I have no idea in what order this might happen, but be assured the order will be the one to most maximize your growth potential.

Increased Psychic Abilities

As you begin to recognize your path and move on it, you will develop little skills like listening to yourself, along with a heightened sense of awareness. This lethal combination will undoubtedly either open up or increase your psychic abilities. If you have ignored or avoided these abilities for a long time they could really explode on you. Your dreams may get more active. You may have so many gut feelings that you think there is a constant earthquake going on. People you know that are now on the other side may decide to speak with you. Your spirit guides or angels might appear to you or perhaps you will just start channeling.

These are all perfectly wonderful gifts that are being shared with you, but you might find them a little unsettling. However, if your purpose in doing this work is to impress, show-off, gain power over someone else or receive external validations for them, then it could easily be the last thing to happen. And perhaps not until you are past the point of needing the external validation or the desire to have someone else's power, will you access them, if you are lucky. Or you may choose to access them right off so you can face all the "icky" stuff that it will force you to face! (By the way, icky is one of the more high level spiritual and metaphysical terms that I am quite fond of using). As you proceed through class work, I will give you some tips on how to avoid experiencing chaos through the emergence of these gifts and how to use them beneficially for your soul's growth.

S-T-R-E-T-C-H-I-N-G Your Comfort Zones

We have all created this nice, safe, little zone around us which affects not only us but also everyone near us. It gives us a feeling of safety or predictability about what to expect from ourselves and most of the people in our environment (family, friends, co-workers, etc.). This zone is your comfort zone. As a child we are constantly expanding and trying new things, therefore stretching our comfort zone. This will usually continue until we are trained to be fearful of what is beyond our field of reality. Some people will spend their whole life pushing their boundaries. If they fall into a traditional form of success they are innovators, people on the cutting edge, explorers, and heroes. If what they achieve is not perceived as successful, then they are fools, dissidents, radicals, troublemakers, and losers. And even those that are constantly pushing will still have those areas or parts of their lives which they will not venture beyond.

As you explore the boundaries of your comfort zone and venture forth, trying different things and seeing the world from a different paradigm, you will change in the process. Growth always does this. At times you will feel uncomfortable and may have to fight not to revert back to old, well established (though not necessarily healthy) habits. Be prepared for your BS to scream and holler at you, "What are you, foolish?" "Why bother with this?" "You were just fine before, you do not need to make changes." "If you do this, your world will fall apart." Remember, your BS speaks to you from fear. Moving forward into unexplored territory is pretty scary, at least for your BS.

Loss of people in your life

As you continue to grow and stretch your comfort zone, guess what happens to the people around you? If they want to stay in your life they have to stretch their comfort zone as well. If they do not, you will either leave them behind or they will become so uncomfortable around you that they will bail out. Think about it this way. How often do you go to friend 'A' knowing what friend 'A' will say? Maybe they will tell you what they have always told you. Maybe they will tell you what you want to hear. In turn, you tell them what they want to hear.

By doing the work in this book you not only see your immediate world differently, but the world in general. Now friend 'A' comes to you and wants to hear exactly what they expect to hear and you say something different. You have just changed the rules and they feel left out or out of sorts. Now, they might be thrilled and supportive immediately, the best-case scenario. More often, however, it will usually take some time for them to adjust, if they ever do. At first, some people may seem to be really supportive, but more often then not I have found those people are in the "This is just a phase" mentality, and are counting on you to return to "normal."

I am not saying that you will lose everyone from your life, but be prepared for some resistance, even if you feel that the changes are only affecting you. Maybe you are just eating better, or losing weight. Maybe you are a more upbeat, positive person. These are still changes and just like your little BS screams at you, their little BS screams at them when it comes to you. Sometimes you are the reflection in the mirror of all the changes they want to make in themselves and are not making.

The hardest part of this whole process is the understanding that if there are people you lose because you are becoming a healthier, happier, person, then it was time for them to leave your life anyway. Other people, more supportive, will take their place. How is that for scary?

Change of habits

As you do this work, you will be asked to challenge all of your habits and allow those that no longer serve a purpose in your life to go away. Now, it is not really that simple, but it is also not the kicking, screaming, dragging kind of withdrawals you may have heard about or experienced in the past.

In the first year and a half of applying these principles in my life, I stopped drinking alcohol, anything with caffeine, stopped smoking and stopped eating anything with meat or meat by-products. In the process, I lost over sixty pounds. None of those things were my goals, and none of those things leaving my life (note - I did not give them up - they left) caused withdrawal. I lost my desire as I lost the need for them. I am also not saying that this is what must happen for you to become more enlightened and to walk your path. Like I said, every person's path is individual. I will not tell you there is anything you have to give up to be spiritual. Also you may find as you detoxify yourself through all four levels: spiritual, intellectual, emotional and physical, some things will come back into your life in moderation, but are no longer self abusive habits.

Limbo

As there are things, people, and thought processes you leave behind, you will most likely have a period where you no longer fit into your old world, but have not yet made your place in your new world. If you are not prepared for this it can be very unsettling. If you are prepared, it may be only mildly unsettling. I have yet to find anyone who makes it through without some unsettling feelings because you are just that - unsettled. The danger here is that you have both your BS and those people who feel left behind (and some actually are being left behind) trying to harpoon and drag you back, even though you know a better place awaits you. You are just not there yet.

Just before this feeling of limbo hits you, will probably feel like a rubber band. You have been stretching just as far and as hard as you can to get to where you need to be, without letting go of where you were. The unfortunate thing about this state is that no matter how far you stretch, you do have to let go, or you cannot take your place in your new world. Sometimes limbo can last a few days, sometimes months or longer. I believe the longer it takes to let go after you have moved beyond that comfortable stretch time, the longer you tend to float in limbo, never quite feeling like you exist in either world. It is different for each person and there are no hard and fast rules.

<u>Hope</u>

For those of you who do not remember the story of Pandora's box, let me remind you of the last thing that came out of the box - *Hope.* For those of you who open Pandora's box, I have two hopes for you to hold on to.

First is the hope for a healthier life on the other side. When I talk about a healthier life, I mean this on several levels. It has been my experience that when you are not in touch with your own connection to the Universe within you, your life tends to resemble a roller coaster, with lots of uncontrollable ups and downs, or maybe fewer but more dramatic ups and downs. You do not pay attention, or perhaps do not even know how to interpret the messages the Universe sends you. Just when you think you are doing well, you get plummeted into crisis, and not with the greatest of coping skills.

As you become more enlightened, a couple of things happen. First, you get fewer crises to deal with because you do not need them to get the messages the Universe is trying to give you. Second, you are much better able to cope with the ones you do get. Instead of jagged highs and lows and a feeling of constantly fighting for the illusion of control, it is more like rolling hills, with gentle ups and downs. As you get more enlightened (enlightened means just that - lightened), there are still ups and downs in your path but you can see them better, which also means that you can avoid them. It's like walking in the dark. If you walk in the dark and fall headlong into a snake pit, there is not a whole lot you can do about it but fight your way out. When you are more enlightened, you can see the snake pit and you can decide either to tiptoe around the edge of it or you may still decide to take the dive, but at least it was your choice.

The other types of healthier include: *physical* - people on their path tend to abuse themselves less, they do not need to; *emotional* - being healthier, they tend to bring healthier people in their life with whom to have relationships, therefore creating better relationships; and *mental* - the attitude with which they face life is better.

The second kind of hope is the ray of hope that you become. As you move to a place where you are the light and are spreading love, light, and healing in all that you do, you become the hope for other people. People who look to get a clearer picture of their own spiritual path will see what you have done as their hope. Remember, it is the spreading of light and awareness which is our only hope to save the planet as we know it, and you can be part of that hope.

Now, let's really get started!

EXPLORING PANDORA'S BOX

Begin with one journaling session about how each of the things which come out of Pandora's Box may affect you: *Increased Psychic Abilities, Stretching Your Comfort Zone, Loss of People in Your Life, Change of Habits* and *Limbo.*

Do each of the first five and write out one set of thoughts which express all your preferences of how things could turn out and then make the second set your worst fears of how they could turn out.

Then decide where you would like to put your energies. Keep that set. Take the other set, bless them, then either burn them or bury them.

PAST

"Those who do not remember
the past are condemned
to repeat it."

George Santanaya
Life of Reason

(Take a number please)

We have had many lifetimes in which our soul has been allowed to participate in many different experiences from many different perspectives. In our soul's evolution, it is important for us to understand humanity from all sides. As you use past lives to give you clues to your current purpose, understand that you may recall or access past lives where you have been a person of many different colors, religious beliefs, nationalities, stations in life, and sexual orientations (asexual to bisexual). You will have been male, female, and androgynous, perpetrator and victim. It is important to understand this concept because how you have handled and dealt with all these different roles will help make up the life that you have created for yourself in this incarnation. Also you need to stay away from judgment, or dog collar terms like good karma and bad karma. Karma just is.

In doing this course work, karma is something that has two states: in balance and out of balance. Picture your soul like a cylindrical object rising up in a tub. As this object ascends, something happens which tips it. It can continue to grow to a certain degree but sooner or later it will scrape along the side and be allowed to go no further until whatever is out of balance is brought into balance. Balance can go either way. For example, if you had a lifetime where you "selflessly" gave to everyone else, a real saint, but had no balance in your own personal life and never did anything to grow, then you are out of balance from that lifetime. Similarly, you would be out of balance if you had a totally selfish lifetime during which you did nothing for anyone else and did not learn from and through your interpersonal relationships. Your ratio of balance and out-of-balance is neither good nor bad, just in or out. If you are out of balance, then you will have the lifetime(s) you need to restore balance.

As you travel through lifetimes, you will do so with different "webs of souls". These souls do not always stay together, nor will the same web be present in every lifetime. The webs will change. Within this web you will switch roles from lifetime to lifetime. Your mother in this lifetime might have also been your child, your sibling, and your mate. The kind of energy you left hanging out there from previous lifetimes will help determine what the energy between you will look like in this lifetime. And it is because of the things that you came to bring into balance in this lifetime that you chose to be together again.

This does not give anybody the right to be a victim or a perpetrator. I have met people who perhaps are being victimized this time around and find that the person by whom they are currently being victimized was their victim from a previous incarnation. They immediately jump to the conclusion that it is "okay" to be the victim and they "owe" it to their perpetrator. That is not what is meant by "bringing into balance". Balance is to have the pattern created and to move beyond the pattern. Whether you have switched roles in the pattern is not the point. The point is that the pattern is not a healthy one for either party and needs to be broken. If both parties do not break the pattern then one or both (depending if one broke it and one just found someone else with whom to live the pattern out) will have to come back to this pattern in yet another lifetime. Always remember, you are only responsible for your part of the pattern. It is not mandatory that the other person in your pattern break it. That is not yours.

When it comes to getting clues from past lives, what you look for as you bring them forward is this: Are there any insights to your current relationships? Is there some pattern that perhaps was made very clear in a past life that you are refusing to identify in this lifetime? Or some lesson you did not learn that you need to learn this time? Or could it be something that you left out of balance that you need to bring into balance this time around?

Often, I will pick up two or three lifetimes in which someone was stoned or burned at the stake for witchcraft, or tortured for unacceptable religious beliefs. These are often people who have a great deal of trouble accepting their power and purpose in this lifetime, particularly if it involves non-traditional spirituality. They are scared to death and yet compelled to explore it, and they wonder why.

We also build clues into our current life to let us know about a past life we might want to access in this lifetime to learn more about why we are here. Those clues can be phobias, or perhaps strong feelings about certain periods of history, races of people, religious ideologies, parts of the world or cultures. Strong feelings can either be positive or negative. The clues can also be a certain ease of an ability, a foreign language, or gift to play a musical instrument. They might even be recurring dreams, feelings of deja vu, or spontaneous past life recall as a child. All of those things are just nudges from the universe to explore our past lives so that we may pick up some clues about our soul's purpose in this lifetime.

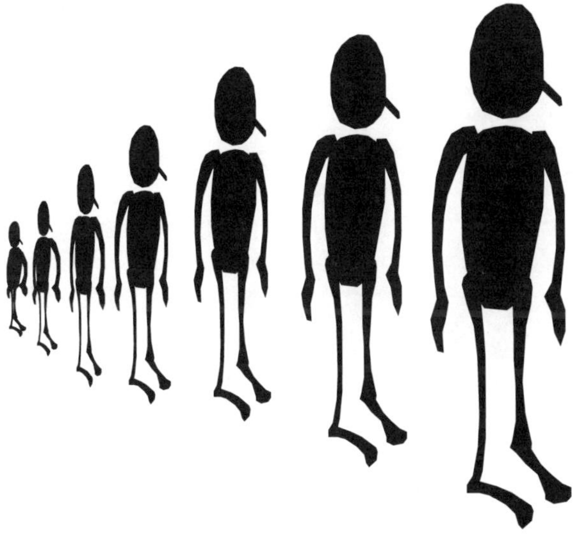

So, exactly how did you create this life that you are in? Well, once you have transitioned out of one lifetime, and considered what you have left balanced and unbalanced from that lifetime, you look at what lessons you have learned and compare them to the ones you were supposed to learn. Then you get help from the master souls on the other side, and you begin planning.

Your plans begin by deciding what patterns you wish to rectify, and which other souls those patterns involve. You also decide which experiences on your checklist you have left to experience. In terms of your past lives, you may want to rectify patterns that you had in lifetimes 436, 587, and 2386. You may check to see if the souls involved with you in those lifetimes, your personal 'web of souls,' have formed again and are currently incarnate. It might even be the same web from all three lifetimes. On a higher level, you then meet with those with whom you want to be incarnate. I do not believe there are any accidental pregnancies, just pregnancies which were agreed to, but of which the mother is unaware. You agree to the pre-determined roles that you will adopt (alcoholic parent, autistic child, etc.) These agreements include conception and birth time. Your soul knows what it needs to balance, feel, learn, and accomplish in this lifetime. Now it is up to you to decode the messages. But, you also have to figure in one small fly in the ointment: free will.

Free will and EGO/BS are "partners in crime," so to speak. We will get the opportunity to do all the things we need to do, but our soul of free will can choose to ignore the messages. We might continue on, EGO/BS-first, into that pit of snakes that we talked about earlier. Being an accommodating being, our higher soul will create the opportunity for us to learn the lesson, over and over and over again, if need be.

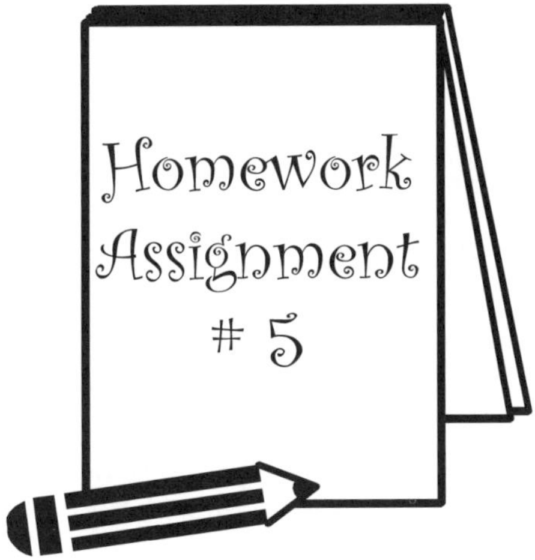

PAST LIVES EXERCISE

If you are interested to see if you can access any of your own past lives, this is the time to get out your colored index cards. First make a list of answers from the following questions:

Are there places that have fascinated you ever since you can remember?

Are there places of which you have been terrified ever since you can remember?

Make a list of any fascination you have had with certain:

PARTS OF THE WORLD
AREAS OF LIFE
RELIGIONS/SPIRITUALITIES
AREAS OF THE WORLD
GROUPS/RACES OF PEOPLE

List any phobias, recurring dreams, deja vu's, unexplained food preferences, unreasonable fear or insights you have to some profession, cultural references, or historic insights which have no explanation within your current life.

Take each thing on the list, starting from the top and write the first one on an index card. Then take the second one; see if it seems or feels to go with the first one. If it does, write it on a card of a similar color. If it does not, write it on a different colored card. Take the third one and do the same thing and so on. Even if you have a match, keep taking the item down through all the cards you have created.

You may find that you have more than one match; if so, write the same thing on your list on more than one card. If there is particular difficulty bringing balance to a specific issue, you may repeat many of the same events from one lifetime to another.

Now take the cards and sort them by color. Then take one pile that you are either most drawn to or one which seems to have the most cards. Over the next week to ten days, meditate on the information, ask for insights in your dream state, and other messages. Also try some outflow writing on the issue, separate from any other writing or journaling that you are doing.

After a week or so, if you feel there is still more for you to get from this lifetime, you may want to read a book or watch a movie closely associated with the time period or culture in which this lifetime took place. If nothing more comes up at that time, just take what you have and do a special meditation or a separate outflow writing.

Ask one night for some special insight as to the importance to your connection to this lifetime - what is its lesson or message for you? How can you improve the life you are living today from the insight you have gained from remembering this lifetime? Then close it down and go on to another one.

This is your life
(and what is it trying to tell you?)

A moment by moment, blow by blow description of your life is not necessary to integrate your lessons and messages from the past. First lets look at the messages you gave yourself at conception. You chose your parents, and what they were/are here to accomplish (and perhaps did or did not), is your running start of getting done what you came here to do.

The next place to look is your time and place of birth. This involves the study of astrology. Because you also chose your time and place of birth, your astrology chart can give you many clues. Any good astrologer can give you your natural born strengths and weakness and the things that you came in to work on. If you have a great many hard aspects or difficult placements, then you probably came in to resolve many issues. If not, then perhaps you came to cover new territory, or bring about change on a larger level. Whatever you came in to do, know that some of the clues lie within your chart. Use your strengths as the ammunition/motivation to get the work done, and your weakness as challenges. You do not have to master your challenges, just bring balance and harmony into the parts of your life affected by them.

Like any great mystery, you may not need all the clues, nor may you be drawn to even investigate all the clues. So if the idea of working with Astrology does nothing for you, than don't do it. It may not be something which is part of your spiritual path in this lifetime. You may become more interested in it later. Either way it makes no difference. Like any other clues I give you, it is up to you to cash in on them.

The next thing to consider when looking into the past is that our veils are usually thinnest when we are children, while we are first developing our communication and social skills. When I refer to thin veils, I mean our abilities to access things like our past lives, our own psychic abilities and our own ELF. Picture your own deepest connection to God as the completely perfect person. This person is physically beautiful, emotionally healthy, intellectually brilliant, and spiritually enlightened, someone who has an answer to all your questions. Now, as you picture this Godlike being, also picture him or her behind a series of veils. The more veils, the more blurred the ability to see and hear this person. If there are enough veils and/or they are thick enough, you may not even be sure that this person exists. On some level you know they exist, but they are so hidden and it has been so long since you have seen them that you start to wonder if this being is just a figment of your imagination.

Our connection to this "being" also has the fewest or thinnest veils when we are small children. This is often when we have our best and closest connection to God and our own higher selves. Oh, by the way, the person whom we see when we get past the veils is the same one we see when we look into the mirror.

The veils get thicker or grow in number through the constant barrage of people and institutions telling us not to believe in ourselves (unless that belief coincides with their version of the world). So as children, we may have spontaneous past-life recall, or we may be drawn to those things that we are supposed to be doing with our lives. As you look back into your early childhood, ages four to six, remember that many things may not be literal translations, but symbols of what we are able to comprehend at our cultural and environmental level. If you put a list together of who you were drawn to read, to want to be, to emulate, look for the similarities and their common themes.

Let's say, for example, you were drawn to Dr. Bombay on *Bewitched.* This could be interpreted as a symbol of non-traditional healing, or even "witch" healing. Now, a five or six year old might not understand the idea that witches were originally wicca, who were the herbalists and the hands-on healers of their time. But on some level this child is not attracted to Marcus Welby or Dr. Kildare, but to Dr. Bombay. Thus, part of your life's purpose might be to be a holistic healer.

Try to remember, or even check out with your parents or older siblings, were there make-believe games you played where you were a different person in a different time period, especially ones about which you were adamant? Perhaps they were not make-believe. These could have been the acting our of past lives that were coming into your conscious mind through spontaneous recall. Not having the skill level to explain this, or trying to and being unsupported by those to whom you were trying to explain it, you could have manifested these memories into "making up imaginary friends or an imaginary life."

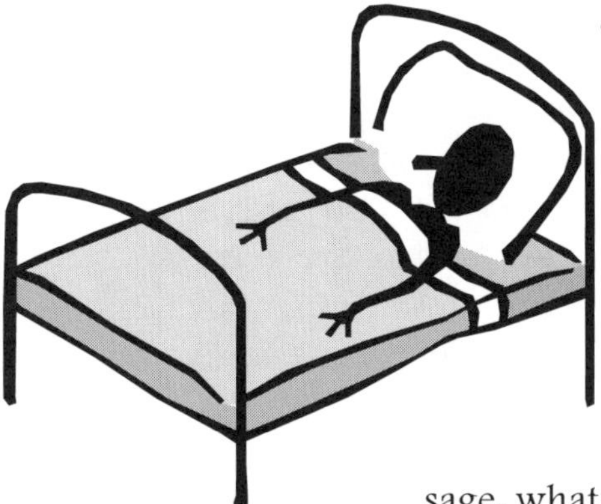

Other things you may want to look at from your past are illnesses and accidents, vivid memories that have stayed with you, recurring dreams, and major turning points in your life. Look at each of these things and try to put to yourself the question, "If this were trying to teach me a lesson, or give me a message, what would that lesson or message be?" Look at what the message might have been to you as a child, or just a younger version of you, and then try to look at it as a spiritual message, a message from your Higher Self or a message from God. As you start to retrieve these messages and lessons, look for patterns. See if some of these patterns still apply today. Are you creating the necessity to keep recreating situations which will give you the opportunity to learn what you have not learned so far? Remember, these messages are never negative, they are not from a place of ego, they are always from a place of ELF.

There are many messages and lessons we have received which can help point us towards our soul's highest purpose, everything from our "accidents" and illness to those things from our past on which we still have energy. Later in the book we will go over how to interpret these messages and link them together.

As you look into your past for some guidance, consider the following tips:

1. *Your past is constantly increasing. Do not draw a line as to either how far back or how current you are willing to look for messages. In this work the full extent of your past includes past lives and comes as far forward as the page you just read in this book. Every time you ignore a part of that timeline, you let clues slip by that can help you find your answers.*

2. *If you have no memories from a certain period of your past, or if something causes great resistance when you remember it, that is probably a good place to start!*

3. *Give credit to the fact that the past is almost all perception. If you bring someone else into your memory search, respect their version as much as your own.*

4. *Do it in writing, even if you never read it again. There is something healing about writing things out. It can be purging. Although the purpose of this work is not necessarily to purge, expect that things will come up that you need to release because they are holding you back. Sometimes you can even do a ritual with your notes when you are finished with them. Either burn or bury them as a symbolic gesture of letting go of what is in your way. This can be remarkably releasing.*

5. *Do your best not to judge yourself or others. Try to remember that, on some level, you brought all these people and events into your life because you needed to*

learn something from them. Beating yourself up, or sliding back into victim mode (or more deeply entrenching yourself into victim mode) will not help the process.

6. Do not let other people invalidate or minimize your feelings about the issues that you remember. If you remember them vividly and to you they were important, look at them from that perspective. Do not minimize them to yourself or to anyone else. This just puts more roadblocks between you and your growth.

As you review your past do not get stuck in it. Honoring your feelings does not give you permission to become a victim, or powerless in your life, because of your realizations. Honor your feelings and then finish the process of honoring them by taking from them the ways in which they have helped you become who you are today and can empower you.

Before we move on, I would like to share something about the importance of perspective when it comes to your past and other people's memories. I was teaching a workshop whose participants included three sisters. We reached a point where the participants needed to discuss their perceptions that they had of their parents and the role they played in their lives, looking for clues to their soul's purpose. Each person had the exercise explained to them and was asked to write down their own experience of each parent. When it came time to read these out loud the father of these three women came out somewhat shaded but fairly close to the same goals, purposes, ideas, and values.

When it came time for them to read about their mother, however, it was so different that one person in the workshop asked if they had come from three different mothers! All three girls did have the same biological mother but just as each day we all grow and change, each girl did have a different mother, in this case a very different mother. When comparing the descriptions with the messages and the individual lives each woman had created, there were some very clear threads. One was a full-time wife and mother, one was a wife and mother but also worked and wanted to juggle both in her life, and the third lived with her boyfriend, probably would never have children and owned her own fairly successful company. Other choices they had made, attitudes they had, and ways in which they remembered their upbringing were clearly linked to this mother - this very different and yet the same mother.

Remember, very often your perception creates your reality. Which of these women had the 'truth' about their mother? All of them! For each one, the truth was clear. As you delve into your past, and as you bring other people into this detective game, honor their perceptions as their truth. Take from them what resonates to you as puzzle pieces for you to put together the picture of your life.

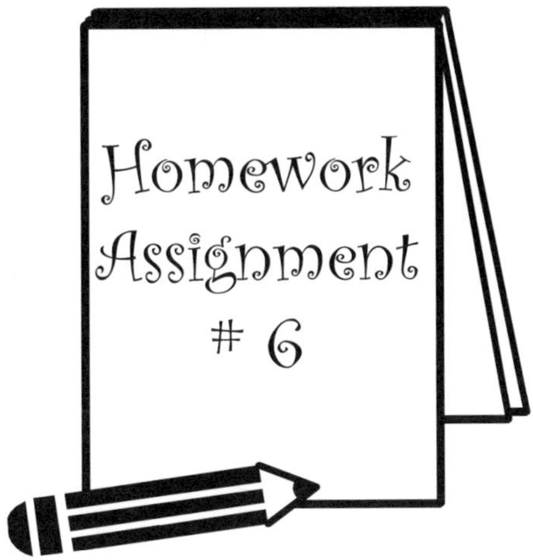

FIGURING OUT YOUR PAST (THIS LIFE) CHOICES

Start here with what you think was the absolute best each of your parents is/was capable of being during their lifetime? This needs to be a positive response. In all the classes I have taught and students I have met, I constantly find one parent who gets singled out. About that parent absolutely nothing positive can be said. If you have problems, I would recommend that you make a list of why you perceive this parent has no positive traits.

What did this parent help you discover, develop, or learn about yourself because of what this parent was or "did" to you? What did you become "in spite of" or to "prove" that you could, because of this parent? What are the positive things about yourself or that you have created in your life because of this parent? Are they things that you would have not developed, discovered, or created if they had not been the parent they were?

Next, examine your perception of your relationship with each parent (or parental figure) and how it affected you. Was there an idea or set of beliefs or principles that came out of that relationship, even if the representation was what you never wanted to be like? Combine the two and then come up with a list of messages you received and/or things you learned. This list must always be presented in a positive manner, since that is the direction in which you want your life to go.

Next, take a look at what the most motivational and positive part of each of your parents was/is and play that out to the highest things that your parents could achieve with their lives, in a perfect world. This is another part of the puzzle of what you are here to do.

INTERPRETING YOUR PAST (PART 1)

Make a list of all the heroes and heroines you had as a very small child. Who did you most want to be like (fictional, historical, famous, family member or local townie, it makes no difference.) Who did you want to be most like or grow up to be?

Then take each person and make a list of the reasons why you wanted to be most like them. Look for comparisons between the list, highlight those qualities or things that are most connected to each other. Have you manifested those traits in your life? If not, then why not? How can you create those qualities or essences in your life today?

INTERPRETING YOUR PAST (PART 2)

Making a list of your past illnesses, accidents, and outstanding events, which thus far have shaped your world, will help you begin to understand the messages you have been giving yourself all along the way. These are not the things that are *supposed* to be important or should be important but those things, when you reflect on your life, most stand out. Then as you look at the list, try to determine what the messages from the experiences might be.

Here are some basic guidelines that you might use to help you interpret those events. Illnesses and traumas which happen to your left side of the body can often indicate either issues associated with your feminine side, receiving intuitive messages, your mother or female siblings, role models, or creativity. Those on the right side could indicate issues associated with your masculine side, taking actions in your life, your father or male siblings or role models, or standing up for yourself. Problems with the throat could indicate problems with communicating, and so forth. Often you can figure out the connection just through using the logical approach of noting what was affected in your body or your life through this situation and if personified, what it would be.

After you have done this, look for repeating patterns and if you are still creating these situations now in your life because you have not got the message yet.

Now . . . make your list. And interpret it!

As you have looked through your past, you may find that you have created a long list of hurts, injustices and things that were just not fair. Now it's time to write some letters. This is not the time to go buy the stamps. I recommend at least four levels of letter writing. On the first level, you write to all those people with whom you still feel energy, alive or dead, still in your life or not. Doing the entire process for each person, one at a time, usually facilitates more releasing and healing. So pick one person and write the first draft where you say anything and everything that comes to your mind.

You can express all your hurt, anger, frustration, maybe even rage about actions they have taken, things you feel they have done to you. This letter may sound childish, unreasonable, even absurd. That's a good sign, especially if the events outlined went back to your childhood. Don't be afraid to exact a little revenge. Tell them what you want from them to "make up" to you for their atrocities. Put the letter aside for a week to ten days. Go back and reread the letter, see from which ones you have already experienced a release of energy. A good indication of the release of this energy may be that you see what you said as absurd or childish. It may make you laugh.

Once you have released the big bad demons from your past, you will find they have little energy left or any power over you to press whatever emotional buttons they did before. It is highly unlikely at this point, however, that you will have cleaned the entire slate. So, compose another letter saying all the things that you either have not had a chance to say or you feel were never heard or honored. The tone of this letter is more likely to be sad, where often the first one tends more toward anger. Put this one aside for two weeks.

After the two weeks reread the letter and see where your energy level is regarding what you wrote. Then read it to see how you co-created the situation. What were the positives out of the experience? Even the most negative experience can be a jumping off place for a very positive trait. Where are you still playing out these traumas in your life? After you have explored all those things, decide what still needs to be said. What current life issues that stem from these earlier issues need to be addressed? Where do you need to set boundaries, take your power back, and change unhealthy patterns? Now write the letter from this perspective. When you write this letter, forgive them for that which they did unconsciously, allow them to be human. Release your expectations of what they should have been, attachments to your hurt over not having the perfect childhood. Remember, if they had known better, they would have done better! Put this letter aside until all your other letters are done. Move on to the next letter.

After all the letters are done, reread all the first letters, honor them (the letters and the experiences) as your teachers and burn them, bury them or destroy them in any ceremonial way which resonates to you. Do the same to each set of letters until you get to the last set. When you get to the last set, decide if it is possible to send these, will they serve a purpose in your life in doing so? If so, it's time to buy the stamps. If not, then create a meditation in which you call in their higher selves, read them the letter, and then let it go the way of all the other letters. Use this same process if the person is out of your life either through time, distance, choice or death. After you have let all the letters go, one way or another, then write a letter to your self - forgiving yourself, for your creation or participation in any of those experiences.

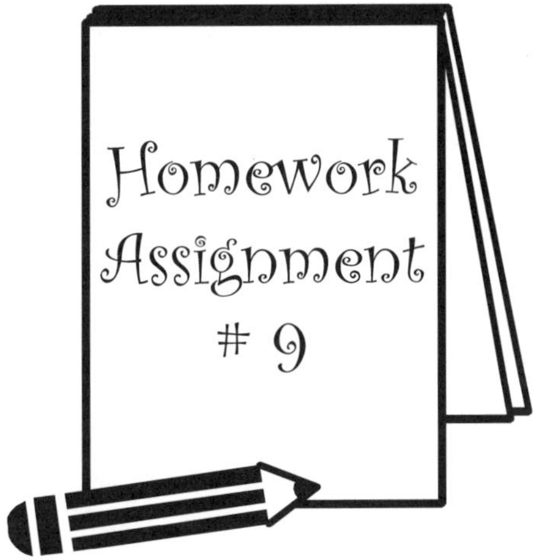

WRITE YOUR LETTERS!

Now it's time to look for the patterns from your past. When I said the word pattern(s), what were the first ones that came to your mind? What was the first thing you thought about that you are really ready to release? Is it your habit to end up in disempowering jobs, or empowering the desires of your parents or children at the expense of your own? Perhaps you repeatedly get involved in abusive relationships. Whatever they are, list all the obvious patterns. Then reread all the homework of this last section and see what patterns emerge. Do you always get sick when it's time to visit your parents, or do accidents happen when you are feeling unloved? Look at all the situations, whether they were between you and someone else or they were things that you did to yourself.

Once you have created this list, it's time to look how these patterns have served you. If they were not of service to you, you would not have created them. Some of these may have developed as a way to survive an abusive situation, or maybe they were the only way you were allowed to get attention, affection, and love. Did this help you deal with a hurtful situation, or is this how you shut down and separated your self from things that you were unable to handle at some point in your life. Whatever the reasons, at one point, these patterns and habits were your friends. In working with many clients, I have found that sometimes these were the clients' best or only friend. It gave them the only feeling of safety, security or love that they ever felt on a regular basis.

I once worked with a client who, when she was a child only received nurturing, positive attention when she was sick. Most of the time, her father was away from home and her mother was simply too busy to pay a great deal of attention. When she was sick was also the only time during which she did not have to serve as peacemaker between her siblings and her parents. As an adult, without fail, she would get sick whenever she went back home for family gatherings and was put 'in the middle' of conflict situations among the people she loved.

Once she recognized the existence of a pattern, identified it and, in this case, learned how to stand her ground and not get dragged in the middle, she also learned how to ask for nurturing support.

By the way . . . she also stopped getting sick.

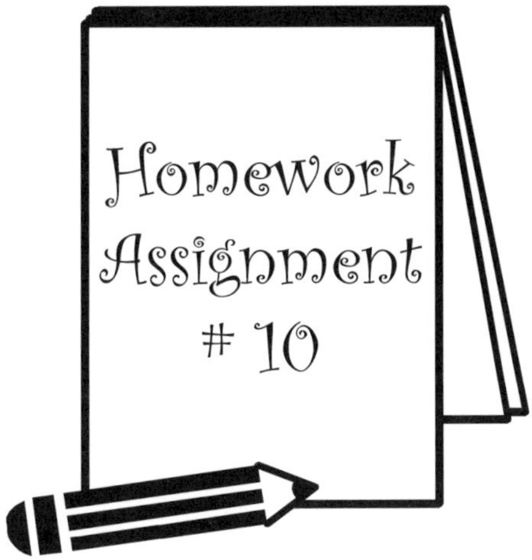

HOMEWORK ASSIGNMENT# 10

Look at the patterns and figure out how they served you at one point in your life. If you are having difficulty seeing the connection, trace them back to when they began. What was going on in your life? What did you need to be saved from at that point? Once you have done that, perform a creative visualization where you picture yourself in some safe, welcoming, beautiful place, perhaps in a garden, leaning against a tree.

Then personify each pattern or habit that is no longer serving you. Have that personification approach you and have a conversation with them. Thank them for being there when you needed them. Tell that you loved them but now it's time for you to move on and say good-bye. Watch as they turn and walk away out of your life. Feel the combination of sadness and joy as you watch an old friend go away, leaving you with a new lighter and brighter life to live.

PRESENT

Definition of insanity:

"To do what you have always done and to expect different results."

The first thing with which you need to come to grips in your daily life is trust. God does not ask anything from you that you are not capable of doing. No question will go unanswered, but you must have patience. You also need to know a few basics, including how to interpret the answers when you get them. You also need to understand if the answers are coming from a place which is for your highest and best good.

"I will know
whatever I need to know
whenever I need to know it."

I first discovered this when I was fifteen. As it came out of my lips I did not fully comprehend what I was saying. I said it in frustration in response to a question that my mentor, Fran Bolduc, had just asked me. Fran wanted to know how I could talk about so many different things, and express so many different opinions about those things, without reading any of the books that she had given me to read. My reply to her was, " I don't know Fran, I just know that I'll know whatever I need to know whenever I need to know it." Now that does not mean that I will know everything, nor does it mean that at times I am not directed to get my answers from books or through conversations. But as time went on I realized how important this statement was when it came to trusting the universe and my own connection to it.

Before we go any further I would like to define the difference between a belief and a knowing. Many people have beliefs. Beliefs are something that you have been talked into and can be talked out of, perhaps not easily, but you can. A knowing is something which a part of who you are, it needs no validation and is part of your personal truth.

Now lets begin by tearing the statement apart and define it clearly. We can then discuss just how important this philosophy can be in your spiritual development.

"I will know. . ."

This is not always something that will come in words. Sometimes you will just feel or sense something about a particular person, place or thing around you but not something that you can verbalize . " I cannot quite put my finger on it. . ." and "I do not know how I know, I just know. . ." refer to this part of this statement.

". . .whatever I need to know. . ."

The main thing here is to look at the word need. Sometimes when I have done a psychic reading, or just in conversation with someone who wants my sense on something and I get nothing, it is because I and/or this person did not need to know the information. We just wanted to know. Wanting is sometimes just the opportunity the universe needs to show you that it does have a sense of humor, though you may not always like it. On more than one occasion I have done a reading for a parent with an adult child who asks many questions concerning the child's relationship, or other "personal" or "private" issues and I will get nothing. Then will turn around and do a session with the child and get a great deal of information about the same areas. It was just not the parent's business to know.

". . .whenever I need to know it."

Sometimes the real question is when. When is it important for me to know this information? There are times when we would do things differently if we were privy to certain information. Through the actions we take and the decisions we make because of that information, we are no longer where we need to be to make a certain reality happen. Therefore, even though you may ask a question or be in search of information on Monday, you may not get your answer for a month of Sundays because it was not time for you to know it.

I had a knowing long before it came to pass that I was going to leave my home and my practice. But no matter how many times I asked, whether it was through asking myself or asking through another person when was I leaving and where was I going, I could not get clear answers. I finally figured two things: One, time is elastic and the when depended on how quickly I cleaned up and finished the work I needed to get done. Two, it was not my time to know. If I knew too much, I might take my focus off staying present in the here and now. Many times when one is focused on what is coming they forget to get what they need out of the here and now. This leads either to being unprepared for the future when it arrives, or changing the future by not doing what you would normally do, thereby creating a different future.

This knowledge has a two-fold importance in your spiritual development: Trust and Inner Knowing. If you trust that the universe will give you the information you need in your life in the proper time and way, allowing you to follow your soul's purpose, then you have won half the battle. We spend too much time and energy worrying about what is coming instead of just being. We must work with what is happening now and learn to interpret it successfully. We get so caught up in the need for controls and guarantees that we miss our signposts, and end up getting lost. Then we have to figure how to get back onto our path.

The other thing we get from integrating this statement as a life principle is that it gets rid of the roadblock of someone else having the way. That we need to find another person, or ideology to get to "Heaven." This is not to say that we do not ever get the answers to our questions or find our sign posts with other people's help, because we do. But we need to rely primarily on ourselves and our ELF to know what to take out of each thing that crosses our path. When we fully accept that we will know whatever we need to know whenever we need to know it, then we can be open to whatever might be helpful to pick up along the way. We do not spend all our time and energy desperately searching for THE WAY.

The first and most important thing that you need to do on a daily basis is to listen to your ELF. Part of this process is differentiating between ELF and BS To begin, refer back to the ELF and BS chart on page 25. You need to figure out whose advice you are getting before you take it.

If you are in a situation where the information you receive is based on the idea of how you can win, then know that it is from the BS part of you. If your information is on how to make a situation a winning situation all the way around, then it is from ELF. Even in playing games you can go in as if the only reason to play is to win, which then sets you up for an emotional roller coaster ride every time you play. With BS, you bet your self-esteem and self-worth. With ELF you play to do the best you can and enjoy yourself. Every time you play, you win by growing through the experience of playing, not by defining your success by the outcome.

Prosperity is always one of the most difficult concepts for my students to integrate. The universe only cuts off your supply when it needs to get your attention, to let you know you are running away from the messages that are being delivered. There is more than enough prosperity to go around. If you receive information from your inner voice that speaks of not having enough, of going without, know that it is BS's voice. As long as you are doing what you are supposed to be doing, the money will always be there. That realization is from ELF.

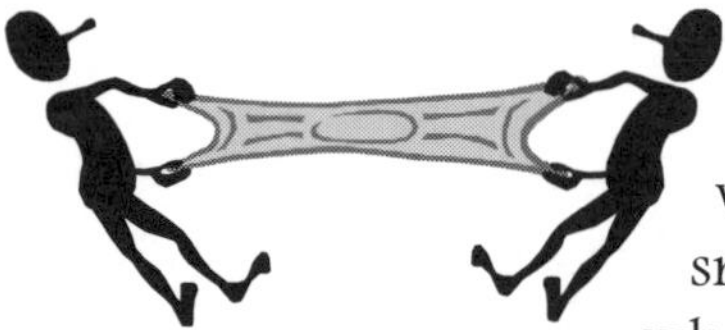

Since I have integrated and lived by this principle, money has not once been a problem, and I cannot say that was true before. People sometimes snicker (other times look horrified!) when I tell them "God writes my paycheck and I do not have to worry about money. God does not bounce checks." If the time comes that I feel money does become an issue, I will know it's not the money that is the issue. My boss is just giving me a warning slip. Now, if I have a problem with money, I know it is a faith or BS issue, not a money issue.

If the messages you receive concern the amount of dislike or even hate that you have for another person, know that this is BS. On the other hand, if you can look at someone and understand that it is the actions you dislike and not the person, then you may choose to not be around them because of the actions. That is ELF.

If you go into a "poor me," or "it is somebody else's fault" mode when things go wrong, know that this is BS. On the other hand, if you can look at those things that are not as you wished them to be and look for a deeper meaning, a message with which you can improve your life, then know ELF is talking.

If you find yourself in "right" and "wrong" mode, saying, "they're wrong, I am right" or "they're right, I'm wrong," understand that you are making judgments and judgments are definitely BS territory. If you put yourself in or allow yourself to be put in a place where you must choose sides, this is not ELF in action. If you can bring harmony into the situation, or at least to yourself within the situation, remembering that we are all one from the same creator, then ELF is at work. Remember the difference between judgement and discernment is that discernment is the realization that something is not right for you. Judgement kicks in when you deem it right or wrong for everyone else!

When thoughts pop into your head, or feelings are just there, look to ELF. Never be afraid to acid test it through the ELF/BS list. If you take those thoughts and/or feelings and start trying to rationalize them, or make a deal with yourself and compromise them, or even feel scared concerning them, then know it's your ECs interfering.

Another particularly difficult BS/ELF battleground for most people is in the area of control. Start with the basic idea that control is an illusion. If you try to control people (spouses, parents, bosses, children, friends, etc.), know that you are coming from a place of EGO. Even if you think that all you are trying to control is your life. How often have you heard the horror story of how an accident, or uncontrolled event shattered someone's life? Before that happened the person may have felt they were in control, only to learn the painful way that they had no control. Things do happen for reasons, and though you may not understand them, as they happen they will remind you again and again that control is an illusion.

If your thoughts and messages come to avoid or fight against change, then avoid or fight against the thoughts. EGO fears change because EGO fears the unknown. ELF embraces change because of the understanding that it is the opportunity to grow and move forward on the path.

If your thoughts and feelings rush you to move on, to be impatient, then it is EGO. It may be EGO trying to get you to run away from that which you do not want to face. If you are still "stuck" somewhere, know that there is a reason, and when you have a certain realization or come to some kind of understanding as to why you were there, then you will move on. These pushes from EGO are personally the most difficult. So, those of you that have problems with patience and allowing things to unfold at the pace that they are supposed to, I understand. I truly do! Why do you think this one was last?

As you listen more to your ELF, letting it guide more of your life, it will become easier to tell the difference. Also realize that it is not easy, nor will it happen overnight. It has taken you the majority of your life up to this point to be "programmed" to let BS, or your institutions of choice, rule your life. All too soon, after you start this process, you will find out just how loud and obnoxious your BS can be, also how deep the programming goes, telling you not to trust your ELF, your Self.

The best way to come from a centered place is to train yourself to respond rather than react. Let us look at reaction first. Reaction is exactly that, re-acting or acting back against someone or something which is acting towards you. It is the easiest and one of the most common ways in which we give our power away. Once we move into a place of defensiveness (reaction), we have already all but lost the battle. Often we talk about how some people intentionally push our "buttons". And the reason they do it (intentionally or unintentionally), is so that we will react and they are much more likely to get their way.

Responding to something is allowing yourself to answer from both your EGO *and* your ELF, not from your BS or your fears. This does not mean that the response is emotionless. On the contrary, it can be quite full of emotions but they are controlled, directed, and personally appropriate emotions, speaking from yourself and not from your fears. However, often if something is said or done which invokes emotions, we automatically go to reaction rather than response.

So when something is said or done which brings up an emotional response - "pushes a button" – and you would like to stop reacting and start responding; try the following:

1. Begin by stopping, saying nothing. Recognize what has happened, that you are out of your center, and take a deep breath.

2. Figure out if this was intentional or if the button was pushed in order to alert you to something of which you needed to be aware.

3. Decide why it has bothered you. If you feel it was intentionally done, then you may want to ask them why they felt the need to push your buttons. This refreshing process has often very surprising results, and will either lead to a productive conversation, further aversion, or someone just dropping the whole thing. Regardless where it goes, you have taken your power back in the situation. If it was unintentional, then examine what you may need to see. You may choose to share your search with the person with whom you are in conversation or take the conversation somewhere else until you can figure out why.

4. If you are not sure if it was intentional or unintentional (and it would be easy to become hurt and defensive), this is a good time to repeat back to them what you thought you heard them say. This gives them a chance to confirm it, or tell you have misunderstood them (which happens more than you think). If they confirm it, ask them what they meant by what they said (in a non-attacking way). Many times people have a different connotation on a word, phrase, or thought process than what you associate with it.

5. If you have clarified what you thought they said, and they said what they meant, then it is time to address whatever issue has been created. You can respond from a place of feeling hurt or angry, or whatever emotions you are feeling. Quite often people confuse being centered with being emotionless. This is not true. For your own well being, it is important to express your emotions and do so from a place of response, not reaction.

Because of the years that were spent silencing ELF to promote BS, when ELF speaks it has a quiet, soft voice. On the other hand, EGO has been taking voice lessons for years to project like a Broadway musical star. Picture the quietest, shyest person you know up on a stage singing a song beside, let's say Ethel Merman or Judy Garland. Whom do you think you'd hear? So, when you are in a situation where you know that your BS (being an expression of your fears) is in full voice, the secret is to put your BS to sleep. You might have certain pieces of music which will quiet the mind. Perhaps a meditation. My preference has always been mantras. Mantras or affirmations, in this context, are statements you create to facilitate changes within your inner being.

I prefer mantras for several reasons. The action of saying things helps release some of the energy that has built up and gets you more involved, taking your mind away from what is upsetting. Music, for some people, can be irritating, even if meant to be quieting. In the best of situations people have a hard time doing meditation, and forget about it if you are irritated! Another aspect of mantras is the repetition. You can say them anywhere from 500 to 1,000 times a day. In student work I develop mantras with my students to help them with their individual growth and to break away from old patterns. Saying mantras is strictly a matter of discipline. You need to say them on a regular basis and "know them cold." In essence, you put your EGO into a hypnotic state therefore bypassing it so that you can find out what you really need to do, or feel, about a situation.

Here is an example of a time when mantras worked for me. Once upon a time I had a life partner and business partner. The two of them had a rocky relationship at best. They would talk to each other pleasantly enough, but they in turn would come and put me in the middle of any conflicts. This might have not been a problem except that my life partner was helping out in the business. It always made me uncomfortable to be caught in the messenger mode because, unfortunately, I felt as though there was never a clear distinction between the message and the messenger.

On one particular day my business partner wanted my life partner to make some fairly complicated last minute changes to a newsletter. As I was driving with my life partner, I knew that if I brought up the changes I would hear all the complaints, and if I let my business partner communicate them it could cause a problem because sometimes my business partner could be less than tactful. So I dropped business partner off and felt myself getting stressed over the situation. I started saying my mantras and by the time I finished saying them I was no longer stressed. It was quite clear to me that this was not my issue. I needed to let the two of them handle it. I needed to make it quite clear that this was not my stuff and I was not going to play referee. Now, this may seem like a clear-cut and logical approach, but in the middle of the war ground it was neither. My students have used this method in both high and low stress situations. You can learn to quiet the mind (BS-based), so you can let your ELF speak.

From my viewpoint, the major difference between an affirmation and a mantra is that mantras are a larger statement of a spiritual belief or knowing, which you are in the process of bringing into your life. For example, "My God is a loving, gentle, and compassionate God," might help if you were brought up in an "angry and vengeful God" mentality.

An affirmation is something you declare about yourself. An affirmation of "I am a loving, gentle, and compassionate person" might be the type one would use if they were feeling that they did not know how to be loving. Many times mantras and affirmations are used together, as you are trying to change what you have been given as reality, and alter patterns, habits and beliefs about yourself which are no longer serving your highest and best interest.

I wouldn't spend a great deal of time on whether you are saying an affirmation or a mantra. It is definitely not as important what you call it but the discipline with which you say it, and what you say.

1. The first step in creating Mantras & affirmations is the commitment to yourself that you will use them. If you are not going to use them, don't bother creating them.

2. Decide what positive things about yourself and your world that

you want to actualize or fully realize and own as your reality. Do you need to create a loving God or a loving view of yourself? How about accessing the world of abundance and getting out of your scarcity mentality? Or is it time for you to actualize someone in your life, to share your life, who treats you the way you deserve to be treated. So what do you want to affirm?

3. Never start with more than three different statements. In fact, I recommend that you start with three. Now you can choose to create three different mantras & affirmations around one issue, or three around three different issues.

4. Now, as you have decided what it is you want to tackle, always put them in the present, in the positive, and the simpler the better. Do not use *no* or *not;* the universe does not recognize negatives so in effect you are attracting the energy to the thing you want to avoid. Also make sure the statements are empowering, no subtle self-criticism in your statements. I have supplied several different mantras & affirmations that I have used, given out or been given, as examples.

5. Start by saying each mantra and affirmation three times, three times a day, at least. If you would really like to effect some change I highly recommend more often. Once you have said them for a few days you should be able to roll them off your tongue. I used to say them when I was driving, especially if there were traffic delays. That would accomplish two things – I met my goal of saying them, and it kept me calm at a potentially stressful time. I would play with mine, linking them together as if they were all one long sentence and say them three times like that, then switch back to doing them individually.

6. Say them for 30 days, without missing a single day! Then it is time to add some new ones. You can choose to tackle completely different things or the same ones, but you need to give them new mantras and affirmations if you are going to keep them. Using the same ones decreases their effectiveness. For the second round, you might decide to do six instead of three. You will find after saying

them for a while they take little time or energy - just discipline, and adding three more is no big deal. If you feel that you still have more work to do with the first set, wait until the end of the second cycle and when you start a new cycle bring back any or all of the mantras and affirmations that you feel you still want to work on. Just make sure you do not use the same ones back to back if you want to maximize the efficiency of doing them. But recycling is always appropriate!

Here are some of my favorite Mantras & Affirmations.

SCARCITY
I am in the infinite abundance of the Universe.

UNATTRACTIVENESS
I am a beautiful divine being.

TIMES OF INJUSTICE
I know there is a just God.

DISCONNECTION FROM SOURCE
I am a radiant being of light

FEAR
I am in the process of claiming my divinity,
in the flow of Divine Purpose.

MANTRAS & AFFIRMATIONS

Make a list of things that it's time for you to work on. Create some mantras and affirmations. Begin the process.

Also, make a list of regularly occurring times when you feel that you have fallen out of your center. Then create one affirmation a month to repeat at those particular times, over and over again, until you feel yourself coming back into center.

There are many ideas out there about what it means to *become spiritual.* For some it means a vow of absolute purity of mind, body, soul and spirit and for others it means transcending to the point of transmuting any self-abusive habits. Either seems extreme to me. As you travel along your path and become more aware of listening to your body's messages, you may find that certain lifestyles or habits will naturally fall out of your life. The key to that sentence is the idea of them *naturally* falling from your life. This is not about "struggling to be pure"; that is trying to live up to someone else's BS of what it means to be spiritual.

Now, the other side of the coin is that this is a good time for you to be testing the waters concerning certain habits you feel to be self-abusive, and you must determine what self-abusive means for you. For instance, if you feel as though you cannot function in the morning without several cups of coffee and you feel you are addicted to caffeine, then it is a habit you may want to examine.

Examining these habits does not include berating yourself or forcing yourself to sacrifice them in the name of your spirituality. It means to identify the habit, make the choice that you would prefer to no longer have the habit in your life, and then to become observant and stay in dialogue with yourself concerning it.

For example, let's examine the habit of smoking. First ask yourself if you are ready to release this habit out of your life. If the answer is "no"- then move onto something else. If the answer is "yes," then begin by journaling about why you think you began the habit. Why did you start smoking? What purpose did it serve in your life at that time? What purpose does it serve now? It must serve some purpose now or you wouldn't be doing it. Keep a log of when you smoke. Divide it into three sections and list how often you light a cigarette:

1) Truly from habit, like first thing in the morning, or when you have a cup of coffee or get on the phone. Look to see at what times you have trained yourself that it is time to light up.

2) In reaction to something that is going on, like, every time your mother calls, but not when anyone else calls? Or every time you prepare for a meeting with a client? Is it when you have to tell your child or spouse something that you know they will not be particularly happy about? Just keep track of what it is that *motivates* you to light up?

3) When you light up for a physical craving, because you are getting a headache, or some other physical symptom?

As you keep track for a few days, you will become extremely aware of the habit. That is the first step to releasing it from your life. Before you move on to any action to help with the movement, take a look at category two. See what life situations push you into "needing" that cigarette. See how you can find ways of dealing with the stress or anxiety to your body, besides being self-abusive. Would it be in your best interest to remove yourself from the situation all together? Is this about setting up boundaries with people who are using you as their whipping post? Or perhaps it's time to stop taking on other peoples' problems. If someone has a problem with you, let them have it. It's not yours. Do not take it on.

After you have computed the log, become very aware of your smoking. Next, all there is to do is to stop every time, before you light up, and ask yourself, " Why am I doing this?" Ask your body, "Do I really need this at this time? Is there something else I can be doing which would be in my higher and best interest in this situation?"

When I first tell people to ask their body if they need it, they always look at me skeptically, as if their body would tell them they needed a cigarette! The fact of the matter is, it may. The idea here is not to punish yourself or put yourself through painful withdrawal. Depending on many different things, you may get some "yes" answers for weeks or months afterwards. Remember to look at how long it has taken to establish any habit you are allowing to leave your life, and do not be so quick to criticize yourself concerning how long it may take for it to leave, in a peaceful, harmonious way.

This structure of releasing can, with minor modification, be used for other habits that you are ready to release, such as caffeine, alcohol, or food. Just insert the correct word and you can use this system. Other things like unhealthy relationships, sex, or abuse can also be used, though they may take more extensive modifications and considerations.

Remember, you will rarely ever get anything to leave your life if you are not ready to get rid of it or if you are not willing to look at why it's been there. And if you do get rid of it, more often than not, you will manifest something to take its place - often equally unhealthy.

One of the keys to this process is to be *honest* with yourself about being ready to allow these changes. Forget about everyone else. So often I hear people who are masters of self rhetoric convince themselves of all the spiritual reasons why they continue on with something to which they are addicted, instead of being honest with the fact that they are addicted and not ready to give it up. And it constantly trips them up, torn between self-deception and self-justification. So, if you're not ready - then perhaps it's not your time to be at that point upon your path. Be okay with where you are and above all, be *honest* with yourself. Lack of self-honesty keeps you from owning the why, and you can never move to the allow, if you do not know the why.

ALLOWING

Make a list of things that you feel you are ready to allow to leave your life. Be willing to accept the fact that up until now they have been there because on some level you felt you needed them. As you make the list, be willing to examine each one carefully and decide which of them you are truly ready to release. Then choose one. Do only one at a time and when you have completed the allowing, take some time to celebrate the movement and when you are ready, begin looking at the list again.

As you look for cobblestones to fit into your path, allow yourself to experience new things. You may choose to attend a Buddhist ceremony or go to a Native American men's council, or women's drumming. As I have moved along my path over the last few years, I have experienced runes, tarot cards, medicine cards, palmistry and a number of other divination tools. I have tried acupuncture, acupressure, Reiki, healing touch, power yoga, regular yoga, massage, deep massage, polarity, ear coning, Inipi ceremonies, sweat lodges, Shiatsu, fasts, herbal cleanses, homeopathy, Edgar Cayce healing remedies, herbology, Tai Chi, European body wraps, holographic repatterning, intuitive primal response therapy . . . and the list goes on. Each and everyone added something to me, gave me something. Some things I only tried a couple of times. Other things I experienced extensively. Some were answers to questions. Others brought up questions I needed to answer. If anything on that list grabs your attention, try it. If there is some form of alternative therapy you have always wanted to experience, then go for it! It might open up a whole new set of clues, or even answers. Stretch those comfort zones.

Remember, however, there are traps out there and times when you may be tested. If you try something, trust your instincts. If it does not feel right or balanced, do not do it again. And if something or someone promise you "the way" or is based on judgment and criticism of whomever or whatever is unlike "them," know that this person or system is not from Spirit. There are fads and cults out there that will play on all your BS fears. Check out what is being said. Does it pass the ELF test? If it does not, then you may really not want to get involved.

It is also important to check in with your own feelings towards the practitioner with whom the work has been done. Sometimes, you can be drawn to something new or different and the opportunity comes up, but there seems to be no connection with the practitioner. This does not necessarily indicate there is anything wrong with the practitioner. It just may not be the right practitioner for you. Every practitioner brings some part of themselves into the process of the work. It is their unique expression of Spirit, so not every practitioner is right for every person. The same is true of teachers. You may know part of your path, for instance, is to study Reiki, and you have met a dozen Reiki teachers, but they didn't seem quite right to you. That is when it's time to wait, in the knowing, that when the time is right, the right teacher, for you, will appear. Also in the case of something like Reiki, where there are levels that you take, you may take different levels with different people. This does not mean that you are saying anything about the teacher you started with when you change teachers. You are simply making a discernment that where you are now is a better match for you.

My partner and I often talk about how we do many more traditional Level Three Reiki training than Levels One or Two. It seems that people really resonate to our book *The Lost Steps Of Reiki*, and want to work with us because of the additional information. The training would be very different with anyone else; not better, just different.

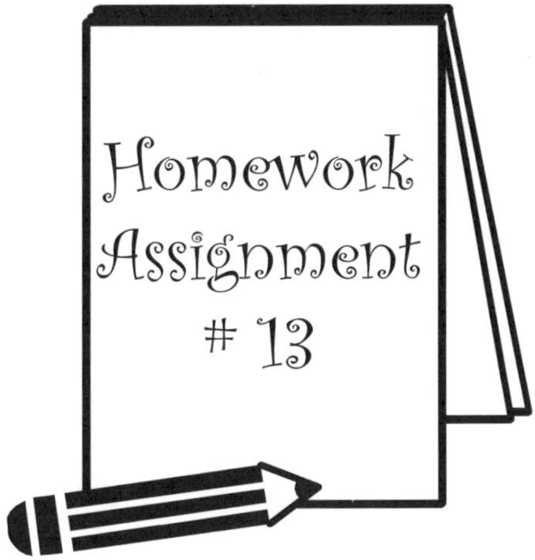

BROADENING THE HORIZON

Make a list of things that you are interested in or would like to try. They do not need to be something that would be seen as "spiritual." This might be a painting class, sky diving or learning French cooking. This is a list of ways for you to be more the person that you want to be.

After you have made the list, then prioritize. Look at the top five things and choose one. Then be willing to take some steps to see if it is something that you truly want to actualize within your life. Get a book or magazine on the subject.

Go to the local library and research it. Find out if there are any local contacts who could give you some first hand insight on it. After you have investigated, decide either to commit to action or move on down the list.

"Working with your spirituality is fine, but remember you have to live in the real world as well," said a friend to me.

"What do you mean by the real world? My spirituality is my world," I replied.

"You know, the world your roommates and your friends live in?" he asked. "You have to live there, too."

"No, I do not." I did not then, and I do not now.

And neither do you. The world I intentionally left behind was BS-based. I created the situation that some of the people in that world were feeling left behind as well. And some were.

What I had learned was to be of the world, not in it. We are here to be part of the world or we wouldn't have bothered with coming at all, but that does not mean we have to be caught in everyone else's version of reality.

You will see the world from a very different perspective as you move forward on your path. I am a firm believer that you need to be part of this world, but being a part of this world does not mean that you still cannot do so and stay true to your higher self. You do not need to give your power away by bowing down to someone else's version of who you are supposed to be or how you are supposed to react. There are several "worlds" within this world. You were born into this world, at this time, for a reason. And going away for fifty years on a mountaintop for wisdom never quite motivated me. It also gave me the feeling that the wisdom spread from someone just coming off that mountaintop would not be very understandable for someone living in today's world. If you cannot say it in such a way that people can hear it, then what good is it?

You do have to figure out what your purpose was in being born into this place and time. But you can create the reality in which you want to live. Choose not to get caught up in such games as, "What will the neighbors think?" or setting a goal to live up to your parent's (or spouse's) view of success. You will never win these games (in Belief System . . . win/lose).

There are two playgrounds out there. One playground focuses on games like King of the Hill, tug-of-war and tackle football.

The other one builds sand castles and sings in jamborees. You can choose your play-ground. You start by doing the things that speak to your ELF, things that build, create harmony, expand your mind, body, and spirit. Then do not allow yourself to be dragged back to those things you know are not good for you. Do not sell yourself the old excuse that you really did not want to, but were pressured by others. As much as that sounds like the kind of peer pressure one would expect out of high school, how often does one hear (or say) very similar things?

Then take a look at your intimate relationships, your career and your family. Are those things dragging you into the playground that you no longer want to play in? If they are, then make changes. This does not mean that one day you wake up, leave your spouse and your job and never talk to your family again. It means you start to change the realities within and watch how the environment will change. If you keep telling yourself it is not possible, then you are right. It will not be because you will not allow it to be.

It's always interesting as I watch one person who is part of a couple go through this process and worry and fret about how their partner will react to their desire to "change playgrounds". When they finally approach their partner, they discover that their partner also wants to change playgrounds and did not know how! For those who find that there is distance, they come to realize the distance was already there. Only now it is the elephant in the middle of the floor that someone is ready to talk about.

These changes do not all happen overnight. You will not wake up the morning after making the decision that you no longer want to play in your old playground and have a totally new life. You may feel like you have a new lease on the old life however, until you complete the process. Like everything else, it is a process!

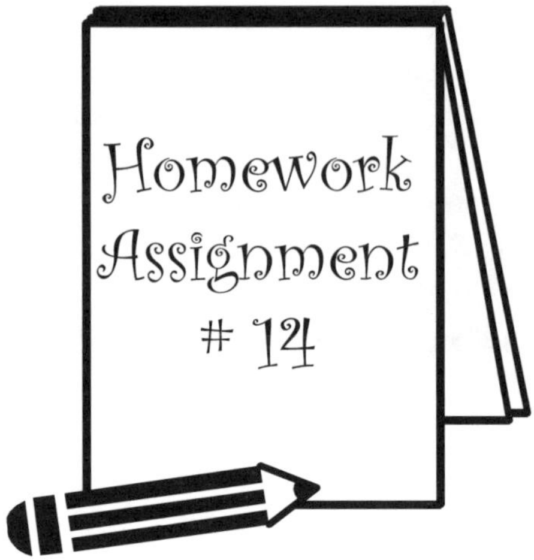

CHOOSE YOUR PLAYGROUND

Make a list of relationships and/or situations which you feel are not in harmony with who you are as a person. What makes them inharmonious? What actions can you take? Are you willing?

As you start this process of re-examining your past, you will make changes in how you live your daily life. Expect that you will have some ramifications that will encompass your emotions, your mental attitudes, and your physical body, as well as your spiritual path. This process ends up as a package deal. You cannot make yourself healthier spiritually without dragging all the other areas into the process. This is what I refer to as integration.

We are not taught to fully integrate the events that have happened in our life. We are fed such things as, "The past is the past; just let it go. That was so long ago, just let it die." or "Do not cry over spilt milk." But in my experience, the past is not the past until you have gone through the process of integrating it. It is like a file that you never closed. No matter how often you open and shut down your computer, as long as you have saved it, it is still part one of your active computer files. It takes active computer memory, unlike a file which is closed and may be even saved on disk. That only becomes active when you need it; it is not taking up active space.

First, go back and start to re-examine your past from a spiritual perspective and try to get an understanding of why you are likely to relive some, if not all, the feelings. This can be very disquieting but it can also be very freeing. While you are on the roller coaster ride of good days and bad days you also will have the knowledge that there is light at the end of the tunnel. Once through this tunnel you will never have to go this way again, at least not emotionally.

You also start to see events and people from your past differently, which means how you see them now is also different. Quite often, as people go through this process, they are amazed at how their longer-term relationships change. This occurs not only in the way you feel and handle things but also in the way you see the people with whom you have the relationships.

If you have had a traumatic event at a young age, quite often you will lose or leave behind some part of you that stops growing. The way that you interact with that person in your life is like the age at which development was arrested. If the event were to happen at five, that is not to say all their actions will be those of a five-year old, just those responses which in some way trigger the trauma. If we have a life filled with many different kinds of trauma then we may be functioning at several different ages in different areas within our life. As you go back and face the trauma and put it into perspective, you can then understand and integrate the experience.

The difference between this kind of work and traditional counseling is that traditional counseling may bring you back to see parts of your past from the perspective of an adult. But it does not try to give guidance to the why of the event in a way which truly closes the door. Many of my students are people who have had years of therapy and find that it leads them to a certain point but then does not really give them the guidance to truly integrate and put the incidents as working parts of their past. It does not answer, "Why did I need this to happen?"

Remember that, in integration, this is not about getting caught back up in the merry-go-round or patterns of the past. Papa always told me, "Never regret. You cannot change something one minute after it has happened. You can learn from it, and do it differently next time. But never regret, it's a waste of energy." Make sure you have closed that file. Do not let your past be your present, and thus your future. Remember that computer file, the one that you saved but never closed? As you opened and closed your computer, it was always taking up active memory, or current energy. What you are doing now is closing the file. It is still there and you can access it if you want, but it is not present all the time taking up current memory.

It is also normal to go through a period during this time where you will get physically ill. It is not uncommon for my students a month or two in to the process to get a severe flu for a few days or a week. As you start to bring this stuff up and let go of it, you also release toxins within your body. As you have painful events occur in your life, the cellular level of your body will store toxins which are produced as a reaction to the events. You might eat a very clean diet, fast or do some kind of cleansing, but until you give your body the green light that you are ready to let go of an event or trauma, that it is safe to release these toxins, they stay in your system.

You do not always need to recall all of these events to have this happen. For example, if you are dealing with some abuse issues from your childhood, you may remember only some of them, enough of them to begin the healing process. Once you learn what you need from those events and you can let them go, the deep level of the de-toxification begins. You do not need to re-live or even remember each and every incident of the abuse. How will you know when you have let a great deal of that energy go and are well on your way through the healing process? When you have a "new" memory or a flashback you will feel the pain or sadness but on a level where you can handle and integrate in a positive and healthy way. You do not get thrown into old patterns or depressions. Congratulations!

Weight loss is often part of the process. The best way to deal with this "letting go" often includes cleansing and body work, at the very least, the drinking of a great deal of *pure* water. Get yourself up to at least a gallon a day, so you can flush your system. The quicker you get these toxins out of the system, the less likely they are to create illness. Quite often, if I have students who are releasing many things from their past, I will have them do a combination of cleansing, fasting, and massage to really help loosen up the toxins and flush them through. And for those out there who feel fairly clean and pure in their diet, I share one of my experiences around the letting go of one of my major traumas.

I was going down to Florida for business and to spend a

month with two friends. Both of these friends ate a fairly healthy diet, but still indulged in things with the normal level of high toxicity found in a supermarket. I was in the process of doing a massage and a fasting cleanse just before I left. During this time period I was having new incest memories come up and I was actively trying to heal some old wounds with my parents, one of whom was diagnosed as terminal. I was also getting ready to move and watching my business expand tremendously, what I call a normal time period in my life. If you wonder if I was stressed, I wasn't really because I had reached the acceptance part of my own spiritual process.

The day before I left I had lunch with a close friend. We were discussing my upcoming trip. As I ate, I received a very clear message, in my head, from my body, and I shared it with my friend.

" I am getting ready to start losing weight again."

"Any plan in particular?" she asked.

" No, I have no idea. All I know is that my body told me that it is getting ready to lose some weight."

My friend looked at me a little skeptically but shrugged her shoulders and smiled, "Okay."

When I arrived in Florida my friends asked me if I was game to do a master cleansing fast with them. Since they do not believe in accidents any more than I do and I was looking to cleanse, it seemed perfect. The cleanse was not set up for any particular length of time. Your body's level of toxicity and the amount of time you spent on the cleanse is determined by the white coating of your tongue. My gut feeling was that I was going to need to stay on the fast for 21 days, which my logical mind (BS) told me seemed long and dangerous. But my gut told me to go for it. Logically, I felt that I would probably have the least-coated tongue after the first day. After all, I had been strictly vegan for over eight months, and regular vegetarian for over two years. I had not had any caffeine or alcohol for over a year , and had done an herbal cleanse three months earlier as well as shorter fasts about every six weeks. I was still holding onto some extra weight but felt the slow weight loss was a healthy sign, 70 pounds in seven months.

When it came to tongue testing time, not only was mine the worst, it stayed that way. It took me longer than anyone else to finish the cleanse. It was a couple of days before I figured out that I had been finishing my integration process from the past, and had poured toxins into my system like it was the Hudson River on a bad day!

So you may laugh, cry, lose some weight, change some attitudes, and feel some old pains. And it is all okay. It is part of the process, and you will feel much better when it is over!

One of the other things that comes up on a regular basis in work with students, is the need to bring balance to the masculine/ feminine sides. There is a major difference between male/female and masculine/feminine. In order to harmoniously balance both sides and be able to draw equally from both sides of the energies, you must first murder the myths surrounding them.

Let's begin by defining masculine and feminine energies. Your masculine energy allows you to complete tasks and undertake adventures. It is your left brain and controls your right side. It is your explorer side. It is also the part of yourself that you count on for physical protection. This energy tends to see things as a logical or analytical progression. To this side of you, 1+1 must equal 2 or it is completely disoriented. Compartmentalization is a key function of the masculine side, keeping things separated. You think one way at work, one way at home, one way with your friends and you do not mix ways of thinking or dealing. This is also your more sexual side, driven strongly by animal instincts for procreation.

Your feminine side is the side which receives more messages from Spirit. It is also your creative side which sees things differently, and your inventor side that likes to look at the world from many different angles. It is your right brain and controls your left side. Your feminine energy is free flowing, letting all parts of your life flow together. It is also the part which tends to keep things more hidden or to itself. The feminine is magnetic, drawing things into itself instead of going out to get them. This side of your energy can deal with many different and contradictory ideologies at the same time and manage them all, not needing to be logical. This energy is of sensuality and pleasure, not purpose-based.

As you look the list over, stay away from associating a negative connotation to either side. Because masculine is logical, does not mean feminine is illogical, and so forth. Look at your own life and see if you are feeding both sides of your energy. Sit down and think of when there might be times to use one side of your energy instead of the other. Think how much more productive you could be if you could call on the correct energy in the correct situation. There is a certain androgyny to following your spiritual path. Do not be afraid of it.

Now its time to look at some of the myths.

Myth #1

A person is all male or all female.

Reality #1

Everyone has masculine and feminine energy. The percentages of those energies will change during our lifetime. The changes occur as we re-focus our priorities, go through traumas, move to new lessons, react to our significant others' growth, and just plain grow older. In different stages of our life we may be more into one side of our energy than the other. It is not uncommon to find a male who had little time or patience for his children, but is the first one who cries at the birth of his first grandchild. In this example, he could be going through the natural transition back and forth of masculine and feminine energy. He could have, in the earlier part if his life, been buying into the myth of what it was to be male and reached a point of wisdom where he no longer had to prove his masculinity. Ideally, we should be able to have full access to both our masculine and our feminine energy at every stage of our life. We should be able to draw from each at any given moment, contingent on what side is most appropriate for our own growth, learning, and understanding of self.

Myth #2

Being more into your energy one way or another indicates sexual preference.

Reality #2

You can be a male very in touch with your feminine side or a female very in touch with your masculine side and it does not mean that you are homosexual. Most people, when they can get beyond the mental reconditioning and the society hype, will have their energy go back and forth from more masculine to more feminine. That could naturally happen several times in a day. If we truly listen to our inner self and go with what we hear, we would find that in each situation we would be drawn to act within the energy style which was most effective in the situation. Often we are so blocked by what it is to be "male" or "female" that we fight those urges or deeply suppress them as "wrong" or "unnatural." What is unnatural is the societal myth of what men and women are supposed to be.

Myth #3

There is a stronger or weaker sex.

Reality #3

Both sexes have their strengths and weaknesses. You more often hear women referred to as being as changeable like the sea and a man referred to as solid as a rock. So which is stronger, the rock which endlessly sits there with the elements beating against it or the sea which relentlessly wears down anything in its way? Neither is stronger. They are both strong in their own way.

Myth #4

Women are givers and men are takers.

Reality #4

Feminine energy is receptive and masculine energy is aggressive. The receptive energy is one that can be sunk down into and is comforting; therefore, women are often seen as givers when it is simply the feminine receptive energy. The masculine aggressive energy tends to build, conquer, and discover.

Below, you will find a chart of differences between masculine and feminine energy. None of the qualities are better than the others. It is a matter of having a place where they are most appropriate. What you should note is that energy is not male/female, it is always masculine/feminine. So be very clear that we all have both energies. Many of the male/female myths were created by a patriarchal society and church that obviously felt intimidated by women and needed to keep them "in their place," thereby creating the myths. The purpose of dispelling the myths is so that you may claim your feminine/masculine power and utilize both in your spiritual growth. Whether you are male or female does not matter. I will not go over the list item by item. A general understanding is all that you need.

Masculine / Feminine Energy Chart	
MASCULINE	*FEMININE*
Aggressive	Receptive
Practical	Creative
Analytic	Free-Flowing
Outer Shell	Inner Shell
Sexual	Sensual
Dynamic	Magnetic
Logical	Lateral

FUTURE

As you clean up your Past and improve your Present, do not re-create your Past by ignoring your Future messages . . . for then you will have to clean yourself up all over again.

As you proceed on your spiritual path the universe has a unique way of giving you loving guidance and direction so that you may continue on your correct path. It is what I call the wrecking ball message. The sooner you learn to detect and diffuse it, the quicker you can maintain that gently flowing pathway discussed at the beginning of the book. The universe will not only provide the lessons for you to learn the things your soul decided you need to learn in this lifetime, but will also let you know if you are headed down the wrong path . . . or maybe even the right path, but just the wrong way.

At first, when the universe wants you to re-examine your path or direction, it will send a little message which always makes me think of a split pea. Remember when you were a child, those little split peas that you use to shoot through a straw? It's as if someone from a distance shot one and it hit you in the temple. It's not really painful, just a little annoying. This is when you continue to tell yourself that you will give yourself some meditation time every morning so that you can feel more grounded and healthier about your self and your day. You will take some time for yourself. But every morning, the kids need something, the spouse needs something and you really need to get to work early and finish a project.

So you get a flat tire, three times in one month, each one

delays you for forty-five minutes to an hour. Do you think, "Gee, the universe might be trying to tell me that the world survived for that time I was unavailable"? Maybe I need to take that time so I do not have to manifest those flat tires to give me some time for myself." Or do you think you are lucky you did not take that extra time or you would have been really late. If this is you, you have just been hit by a split pea.

If you still ignore what you need to do, then you get the marble thrown at your back. The very next week you have a fourth flat tire, but this time you try to change it yourself (the tow truck takes too long) and you throw your back out and are laid up for a couple of days. Flat on your back, bed rest. Now, are you re-examining your priorities or are you lying there trying to figure how you can catch up? If you are figuring how to catch up, the universe has a present for you!

Baseball anyone? Upside your head at close range. Now you are driving too fast, running late, because you have overcommitted yourself and you have an accident that lands you in the hospital for several days and the car is totaled. You spend all your time figuring out how you are going to catch up. So you decide to go against doctor's orders and go back to work early.

You're up and your next sport is bowling with a bowling ball knocking you off your feet. You go back to work to early, complicate the situation and end up back in the hospital for six weeks. And if you are still in denial about the need to make some life changes, then you get what I call the big wake-up call.

The big wake-up call is when you open up the door one morning to find you are trapped in the doorway and a New York wrecking ball is headed directly for you. This could be anything from diagnosis of a terminal illness to a heart attack. Maybe your partner (who you thought was happy) walks out on you. Whatever it is that hits you, it is a life-changing or life-shattering event. It is the kind that makes you cry, "Uncle!"

The wonderful thing about getting

on the right path is that the universe will provide for you. I will not say that everything is suddenly champagne and caviar. But the things you need to accomplish will manifest themselves and you will feel better.

So, unless you have what I call the Phoenix complex (crash, burn, and rise from the ashes to start all over again), wake up and pay attention to what the universe is trying to tell you. And oh, by the way, it was the New York wrecking ball that hit me which landed me doing what I am doing now . . . what I should have been doing all along.

At times people ask if I am espousing the theory of an angry and vengeful God. The answer is "No," because God did not do this to you. You manifested in your own life the experiences you needed to get the point! And you are extremely loyal to yourself and will keep speaking to yourself until you listen. No space for victimhood here. Also, you may have noticed that the events seemed to get closer and closer to each other. If you are really in denial about something, especially if you have verbally identified it but taken no action to rectify it, it is often true that the messages not only get louder, they get closer.

GOOD LUCK! STOP, LOOK, AND LISTEN!

WRECKING BALL

Every day, for three days, keep track of all those little (or big) events that seem to annoy you: the accidents, the coincidences, things that you perceive as undesirable. At the end of three days, look over your list. See if you can figure out the messages that you were trying to give yourself. Think back to what was happening at the time, any feelings you were having or any problems you were pondering. See if there are adjustments you can make which will alleviate the necessity of having to have a louder message given to you. Do this exercise once a week for a month. Then try doing it on a daily basis, for a month. Finally, try doing it as the things actually happen. At this point, you are not stopping to write anything down - you are doing the analysis on the spot.

As you move along your spiritual path, look for the signposts and clues to your direction. And when you want to know something, just ask! That may sound very simple - too simple to some people - but it works. The secret is knowing how to ask, how to listen, and how to interpret what you hear. There are also two minor catches. You have to be willing to trust the information and you have to do something with it.

In all of the years that I have done psychic readings for people, you cannot imagine the number of times people would either ignore the messages, fight me on them, or try to twist those answers to fit the answers they wanted to hear. The other thing I would hear regularly was that I did not tell them anything they did not already know. They just did not trust themselves enough to believe in the answers or guidance they received. It was easier to believe in a stranger. That, again, comes from our conditioning. If we listen to someone else then we do not have to take responsibility for the decision that we made- they told us to do it.

The first secret is how to ask. Begin by knowing exactly what it is that you want to ask. Be clear in the question. Do not ask multiple choice questions. I am not saying that you will not get an answer but yes/no questions are hard enough to interpret without having a multiple choice. Be prepared to ask more than once. Ask in a serious meditative moment; perhaps when you do your morning and evening prayers or affirmations. Ask not only twice in the same day, but ask two to three days running. DO NOT ask from a place of plea-bargaining. Such as "If you just give me this information I will never do so and so again." I find those questions take the longest time to answer because they are from a space of fear and EGO, not high on the priority list from your spirit guides. Also make sure that your question is from a place of ELF, not BS. You may find that if you ask a BS question, you will get a BS answer.

Now that you have put the right question out there, sharpen your awareness skills and brush up on your foreign languages. No, not Spanish, French or German. This is the Universal language.

There are many languages spoken within the universe, and when you ask the universe a question it may answer you in many different languages. Learning to be aware of the different ways that the universe may answer you is a wonderful developmental tool. Just as one might learn Russian, Dutch, or Italian, one needs to learn the many forms of Universal. This is one of those Catch-22s. You cannot get and interpret your messages from the larger universe unless you move out of your own BS-centric little universe.

DREAMS

Dreams are a common Universal language. In your dream state you put your critical mind (BS) to sleep and your intuitive mind (ELF) can communicate. Even within the dream state there are a variety of different ways in which you might be addressed.

You may have dreams that are more like memories. Sometimes a character in a dream is you, but you look different. Perhaps it is you but you are in a place or time which, while seeming familiar, is not in your current day awareness. This kind of dreaming could be past life dreaming, a soul memory which your conscious mind will not let you enter. Just because it is a past life, do not dismiss it as unimportant to what is going on in your current life today. Perhaps there is something tied up in that past life which is an answer to the question that you asked concerning the life that you are living today. Record that past life and see how it fits into the past life exercises which you did in connection with the earlier chapters. Question if there was something from that lifetime that you need to rectify or the answer to some fear or phobia that you have today.

The second kind of dream may be clairvoyant, a glimpse into the future. Remember that the future is not written in granite. Perhaps there is something you can do to change the future that you saw about to happen. Sometimes there's not. Also keep in mind that when you are dealing with things like clairvoyance you can sometimes end up in a no-win situation. For example, you dream that your best friend will be in a car accident the next day. You call your best friend and tell them. The day goes by and it does not happen. You feel relieved but you also feel foolish. You must remember that maybe because you told that person, they drove more carefully and that is why they did not have the car accident. Another scenario is that you did not tell them and they did have the car accident and then in some way you feel responsible. Trust yourself.

The next kind of dreaming might involve flying dreams or dreams of being somewhere else which feel as if you were actually there. Guess what? Maybe you were! It is not uncommon to have out-of-body experiences in your sleep.

There is also a type of dream where you are in a classroom. You may have been. There are classrooms to which your soul may travel. These are, in essence, happening on other planets or other dimensions, where our souls are learning lessons on a higher level.

The last kind of dreaming is the one we will most commonly remember and it will happen in symbols and often in many acts. We may be an observer or a participant. This is where the most common answers to our questions come. Look at each section of the dream and try to break it down as to what the individual components represent to you personally, and what each person in the dream represents as an aspect of yourself. This could be something you have in common with someone in the dream or sometimes what that person possesses or represents that you most would like to develop in yourself.

In some instances, we may be able to stop and start the dream or make changes as we go along. This kind of conscious interaction is called lucid dreaming. Lucid dreaming often depends on how advanced we have become within ourselves to take a controlling role in our dream state. Here, we may be able to interpret the dreams while we are dreaming. Or even control the outcome of a dream.

If you feel that you are getting a great many answers in your dream state start interpreting your dreams. See the homework following this section for advice on how to create a dream interpretation log book.

COINCIDENCES

Since there are no accidents and no coincidences, if you are asking for answers to something and the same thought or recommendation keeps coming up, then perhaps you should look at it a little bit closer, or follow through on the recommendation. Sometimes I call these pushes.

An example of a push occurred recently to someone who had come to me for a consultation. It seemed that my role was to be the first push. During the consultation it came to me that it would be particularly helpful for her to read a certain book. I sensed that if she read that book, things would start falling into place for her, so I recommended it. The woman attended a workshop that I taught a couple of months later and filled me in on the rest of the story. It seems that a few days after seeing me, she received a phone call from a friend of hers who was reading the very same book. This friend encouraged her to get a copy of the book, but the woman still resisted. A week after that, another friend of hers came by and dropped the same book off to her, said that she just had to read this book and offered to loan her copy. My client let the book just sit there for a couple weeks. Her friend who had read it called and asked her how soon would she be finished because she had a couple of other friends who wanted to borrow it. My client told her that she just had not had the time to read it and to pick it up. She would borrow it later after everybody else had borrowed it. A week later she went into a bookstore and noticed that the book was displayed, but she was still being resistant. She went to the section of books that she wanted to browse through and accidentally knocked against one of the bookshelves. A book fell off and hit her. Guess what book it was? She finally bought it! She even read it!

Now before you laugh or criticize this woman's resistance to the message the universe was trying to give her, stop and think about how clear things have been to you in hindsight. The moral of the story is this: if you are going to ask for answers to questions, be willing to accept the form of those answers, no matter how unconventional.

PEOPLE

Sometimes when you are really lucky you will ask the universe a question one night and the next day you will get the answer in a casual conversation. It could even be with a complete stranger. Your answer could be waiting right there for you to pick up on it. Once you ask the universe a question, start listening.

MUSIC / MEDIA

Once you open yourself up to the reality of getting answers this way it can be quite fun. It may be a song that just seems to grab your attention on the radio, or the one that was playing when your radio/alarm clock went off. It could be a song that somebody is just dying to play for you. The same thing could occur if you just happen to catch the tail end of an old movie, or flip channels and catch a particularly intense episode of a show that you do not normally watch. Expect the unexpected.

MEDITATION

There is also the old fashioned way. You meditate and allow the universe to speak to you directly. The problem with this however, is twofold. First, if you have not really learned to distinguish ELF and BS, this is a prime time for BS to sneak in its "two cents." Second, when God does speak, if you are not experiencing trust in your own connection with Spirit, you usually will not believe it anyway. Quite often when I work with students about asking questions, I always remind them that it is highly unlikely that they will get the answer in the direct method. That would be like Moses coming off the mountain with the tablets and in the tablets would be inscribed, "The answer to your question is. . ." You are supposed to be growing and developing new skills. Besides, you would probably want ID and would not believe him even if you received it!

SUDDEN REALIZATIONS

This is my favorite. You ask a question and you get a sudden realization or sometimes a voice in your head with the answer. It is nice, clean and quick. But again, if you are still up to your eyeballs in BS stuff, do not hesitate to put the message through the ELF/BS checklist to make sure that it comes from the right place. It always amazes my students when I finally convince them to try this method and it works. All you do is ask the question, make sure you have given up any energy on what the outcome is supposed to be, be quiet and listen. It really works.

So now you know the basics of speaking Universal. The Universe will not limit itself to these ways, but this should give you some ideas. So what are you waiting for? ASK!

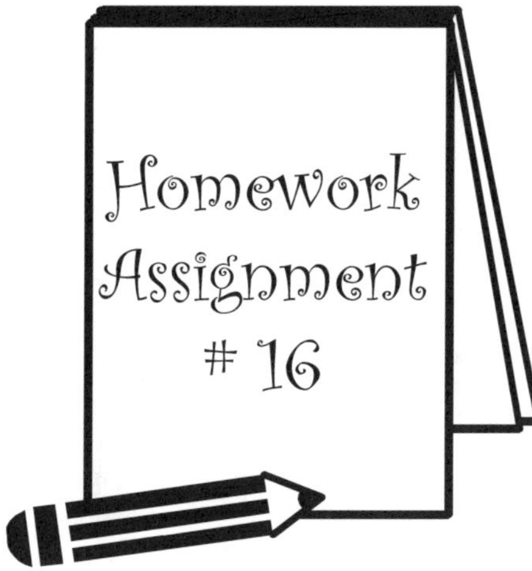

Just Ask!

Begin the exercise by making a list of yes or no questions. Keep the questions simple. In the beginning, the idea is simply to identify, recognize and gather confidence in your own ability to get answers. So take your list and start at the top (or the most time sensitive one). Then ask one question, at least twice a day, first thing in the morning and before you go to bed, and any other time it pops into your head. Do this every day for three days. Then pay attention. Keep a journal of the things that stand out to you for the next three days. At the end of the three days spend some time looking over what came up and see what answers appeared. Try doing one of these questions once a week for several weeks until you really feel as though you are getting answers quickly and recognizing them immediately as your answer. Then you can move on to more "difficult" questions, either those more complicated or questions to which you have more resistance.

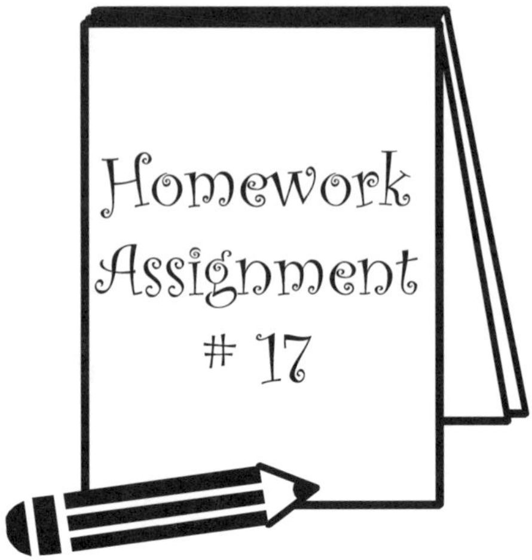

PERSONAL DREAM SYMBOLOGY LOG

In creating your own symbology log, the first thing to remember is, more often than not, the people in your dreams are aspects of you. Though not always true, it's best to start with that interpretation. As you become more proficient at dream interpretation, you will have a knowing if your dreams are a message for someone else. Now remember, this all applies to symbolic dreaming, not past life or clairvoyant dreaming.

As you look at dream and figure out what aspect each person is of you, write it in your log. Each place in the dream indicates a temporal place in your life. Each time or season in the dream indicates a time or season of your life. Write these in your log.

Some symbols seem to have a cultural meaning. If these apply, place them in your log:

left side = feminine energy issue
right side = masculine energy issue
water = emotions
stormy weather = unsettled feelings
current house = the present
old house = message from that period in your life
car = physical body

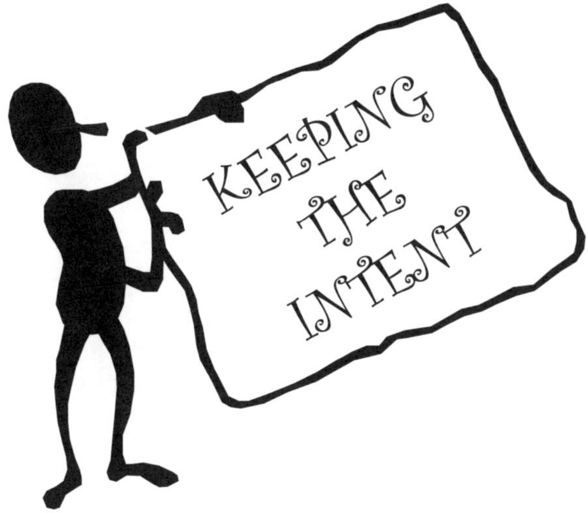

As you get ready to move forward on your spiritual path, the one thing that you do need to keep focused on is your intent. It took me long time to figure out just how important intent was in doing this work.

In my twenties I lost sight of the fact that I was here to do God's work, which meant living my life in a place of joy. I found that what I wanted to do was to make the people who came to me happy. I did not want to see them upset or suffering. This was not a conscious change, per se. It just happened. But the result was that, instead of giving people the information they needed to take control or change their life in a positive way, I was doing little more than mind reading. I would sit there as they came to speak with me, and I would think, "I would really like to make this person happy" All of these wonderful things would start coming to me, the things they wanted to hear, not what they needed to hear. Again, it was not what I was consciously trying to do, but the Universe was providing me just the information that I was asking for - something to make them happy.

I am very clear now that my intent is to facilitate healing. As I sit down with each person, they will hear me say, "I am a healer, and only a healing energy will come to me and through me."

So as you move forward and start asking for Spirit to speak with you and through you be clear on why you want this information. What is your purpose? What is your intent?

As you go through your life and look to work with people who are to be your teachers, ask them their intent. What is the purpose of them doing what they are doing? If they are not clear on this, then it is likely the information you get will not be clear either.

Also look see to if they are stringing you along. Are they giving you insights and realizations that are helping you move forward in your life or are they just telling you enough to keep you coming back, again and again for their insights and wisdom? Dependency is never good. Remember this as well, if you start working with other people or have people that come to you for insight. Do not look at developing this gift as a quick and easy way to make money, for one way or another there is a price to be paid for it, by you. There is nothing wrong with being compensated for your time and talent. However when the acquiring of money supersedes what is for your clients (and your) best and highest good, it has a way of back firing on you.

As you move forward and you are drawn to share what you have discovered, remember not to hold onto the ownership and responsibility of your information. The only responsibility you have is the delivery of that information. It is not yours to give, it is the Universe's. It is, however, yours to deliver. But it is not yours to make sure they accept your truth as you heard it . . . for it might not be THEIR truth. Never feel as though you have wasted your time if it does not seem as though they have taken it to heart. This is the process I call watering the land.

Picture in your mind a very dry and barren piece of land where nothing may have grown for years. You know the potential is there. All the right minerals are in the soil. All that is missing is the water. Now picture yourself standing over that piece of land steadily pouring water onto the land. Pouring, pouring, and pouring until you have flooded the land and it becomes a mud hole or perhaps even the beginning of a swamp. Do you think that would be productive?

Now picture that same piece of land as you originally found it and you pour just a little water on it. Then you let it settle and pour just a little more water on it. Then you are called somewhere else but you know that on some level God has made a promise to do everything possible to make this land fertile. So you move on from this little piece of land and you wish it much love, not cursing it because it was not ready to grow yet, nor telling it you are disappointed in it. You just bless it and move onward.

Later you come back to this little piece of land, and in your absence many other people have lovingly watered it, giving it seeds, and tended to its care. You do not know how many. It makes no difference. But upon returning you find a beautiful garden. You feel joy because your little bit of water and love at the beginning was just as important as the last person who may have just weeded the garden before you got there. You do not feel sorrow because you were not there to plant the first seed, encouraging it to grow. Everyone who worked in the garden was important. Maybe you never got back to the piece of land that you first put that few drops of water on, to soften it, but you are okay with the fact that you did what you needed to do and the rest of it was in God's hands. The other thing to be clear about here is the importance of releasing any expectations that you may have about the possible outcome of the work you did. If you were convinced the land was to be a rose garden, you may end up disappointed. You may also have a negative impact on how well or quickly the land produces. For if, in the scheme of things, it is best for the land to be an herb garden and you keep pulling them out because they are not roses, well, I am sure you see what I mean. Do as you are drawn to do, without expectations and allow the results to be what they are. You will find it better for you and better for the person or situation with which you are dealing.

Recently I went to spend time with a student of mine who has moved into the place of a teacher and practitioner herself. Someone with whom she had been working had decided to have a session with me when I was in town. Later my student shared with me her frustration, as her student went to her after our session and was ready to take some actions and change some things which had been keeping her from moving forward. My student was frustrated because she had been pointing these things out to her client for several months and the client had either denied or ignored the recommendation. Now she was suddenly impacted by my insights. I shared with my student how watering the land works and that if she had not been doing so for the last couple of months, I couldn't have had the impact I had so quickly. I assured her that there would be times that she would get to be immediately insightful because someone else had been watering the land.

As you move forward on your own spiritual path and you look to share your discoveries, look at them as watering the land. Do it gently and do not force your discoveries. Think of how you feel when someone tries to force something on you. Leave your dropper full of water and move on.

Finally, we come to combing the mirror. As you move forward and see the world around you, do not try to do. Just be. Remember, the world that you have created is the one that you need to have in order to learn the things there are for you to learn in this lifetime. If there is something that you need to learn from it, it will be there.

If there is something in your world that really bothers you or that you do not like, find out what it represents within you that you need to change. Change within your being. Do not waste your time trying to change the world on the outside because it will not change. Not really. It might look a little different , but it will be the same until you change the need that is inside of you. We are all trained to try to change something, to fix something outside of ourselves. It makes us feel productive. The only productive thing that we can do is to acknowledge those blocks, fears, unresolved issues, or inconsistencies that lie within us. Deal with them and then we will find that our world will change.

I was once working with a brother and sister. As small children their mother use to take them aside one at a time and tell each one of them that they were her favorite and how much better they were than the other one. Then one or the other child would see mama all affectionate and loving with the other one and feel, on some level, that they had been bad and needed to win back their rightful place. The brother was the older one and learned early how to become very manipulative to win. The sister learned to lie to win back.

They both grew up and went on to live their own lives, but somewhere the message had registered that one needs to manipulate and lie to guarantee your place in your loved one's affections. Ultimately, what was important was to compete and win.

When I met them, the brother had gone through three marriages and had a habit of attracting women who clung to him, allowing him to feel superior. He would get caught in pleasing his families (all had children), his current relationship and himself, and would manipulate accordingly. He was currently involved with a woman who would not buy into that, although at times she would admit to "getting sucked in" and needed to keep her distance.

The sister was on her second marriage and was constantly triangulating between her daughter from her first marriage and her second husband, her mother and her family, and between her brother and his kids. The children seemed to take turns being estranged from their father (her brother), sometimes his own fault, sometimes from his sister's interference and stretching of the truth. She still had a hard time being honest, especially if she felt under pressure to perform or win.

The brother and sister had started a business together shortly before I came into the picture, with their mother loaning them the money. This took them back to the original triad, but unfortunately mother decided it was her time to become frail. She was unable to cope and ended up in a nursing home. She was not going to be able to fully play the third role so that these two could once and for all learn their lesson and put it behind them. Conveniently enough, they hired a third person for the business. They discovered within a few months that he was very good at what he did, and in their perception, was needed. But he also was very manipulative and lied. He would alternately buddy up to one, while trashing the other. They soon decided to sell the business. Guess what? Nothing seemed to go right. It was almost as if they were stuck with the business. No matter how hard they thought they were trying, they could not quite meet the goals that they needed in order to sell. But once we started talking about how this man was representing everything that they had not yet dealt with from their childhood, it became clearer and clearer to both of them what they needed to face and resolve within themselves. If they did not resolve it and still managed to sell the business, something else would just come along that would put them in the same situation until they learned this lesson.

Now they were well on their way to changing their environment. I refer to this as combing the mirror because in a conversation with the brother, trying to explain the nature of change, I came up with this was the exercise to illustrate it.

The next time you want to change, or fix your environment, go to a mirror and mess up your hair. As you look at your messy hair, take a comb and start combing the mirror. Do that for as long as you need to until you realize that no matter how long or hard or consistently you comb the mirror, your hair will still be messed up. Then stop and think about what you are trying to change or fix in your environment and maybe, just maybe, you will decide that it is time to stop COMBING THE MIRROR.

No more than there is truly an end to life is there truly an end to this book - only a limit that my publisher would let me write under this one title. If I have to sum this book up in the simplest of terms I would do it in the following steps:

1. Stop being a victim. You have a choice.

2. Start figuring out the messages and lessons that were being given to you through events in your past, especially those which create victim mode or any other mode which no longer serves your highest and best good.

3. Get up every day and know that you can have a good day or a bad day. It is your choice.

4. Learn how to listen and follow the instructions through your own connection with God, The Universe, Christ, Buddha, Spirit, the White Light, and/or the Great Pumpkin.

5. Get yourself moving within the rhythms of that Universe and stop looking for someone else to give you "The Way." Make it for yourself.

6. Be more enlightened and you shall be more empowered.

7. Release your fears and they shall release you.

8. Do not judge or criticize and do not be judged or criticized - We all have our own path we must walk.

9. Change the inside and the outside will change itself.

10. Be nice to the other people in the world, to all living things, and to God, and you can do all of this while still being nice to yourself!!! IT CAN BE DONE.

Namasté,
Kevin

LightLines now offers individual
Combing The Mirror™ Coaching Sessions

Contact us today to have Kevin (or someone trained personally by Kevin) as a spiritual coach. Your personal coach will help you apply the homework exercises in this book, as well as developing new exercises specifically geared towards your individual needs.

For more information, please call, write or e-mail:

LightLines - CTM
One Middle Street
Portsmouth, NH 03801-4301

(603) 433-5784
coaching@weboflight.com

Other services available from *LightLines* include:

Past Life Regression
Astrological Charts and Interpretations
Dream Interpretation
Intuitive Sessions

All services are available in person and by phone.

And please visit our website at
http://www.weboflight.com

Let us help you stop

Combing The Mirror!